Social Life
and Issues

CONTEMPORARY NATIVE AMERICAN ISSUES

Economic Issues and Development

Education and Language Restoration

Media Images and Representations

Political Issues

Sacred Sites and Repatriation

Social Life and Issues

Social Life and Issues

Roe W. Bubar and Irene S. Vernon
Professors at the Center for Applied Studies
in American Ethnicity, Colorado State University

Foreword by
Walter Echo-Hawk
Senior Staff Attorney, Native American Rights Fund

Introduction by
Paul Rosier
Assistant Professor of History, Villanova University

CHELSEA HOUSE
PUBLISHERS

CHELSEA HOUSE PUBLISHERS

VP, NEW PRODUCT DEVELOPMENT Sally Cheney
DIRECTOR OF PRODUCTION Kim Shinners
CREATIVE MANAGER Takeshi Takahashi
MANUFACTURING MANAGER Diann Grasse

Staff for SOCIAL LIFE AND ISSUES

EXECUTIVE EDITOR Lee Marcott
EDITOR Christian Green
PRODUCTION EDITOR Bonnie Cohen
PHOTO EDITOR Sarah Bloom
SERIES AND COVER DESIGNER Takeshi Takahashi
LAYOUT EJB Publishing Services

First Printing

9 8 7 6 5 4 3 2 1

Library of Congress Cataloging-in-Publication Data

Vernon, Irene S., 1955-
    Social life and issues / Irene Vernon and Roe Bubar.
       p. cm. — (Contemporary Native American issues)
    Includes bibliographical references and index.
    ISBN 0-7910-7971-6 (hard cover)
    1. Indians of North America—Social conditions. 2. Indians of
North America—Social life and customs. 3. Indians of North
America—Health risk assessment. 4. HIV-positive persons
—Medical care—United States.   I. Bubar, Roe. II. Title.
III. Series.
E98.S67V47 2005
305.897'073—dc22

                                        2005006415

Contents

Foreword

Walter Echo-Hawk

N ative Americans share common aspirations, and a history and fate with indigenous people around the world. International law defines indigenous peoples as non-European populations who resided in lands colonized by Europeans before the colonists arrived. The United Nations estimates that approximately 300 million persons worldwide are variously known as tribal, Native, aboriginal, or indigenous. From 1492 to 1945, European nations competed to conquer, colonize, and Christianize the rest of the world. Indigenous peoples faced a difficult, life-altering experience, because colonization invariably meant the invasion of their homelands, appropriation of their lands, destruction of their habitats and ways of life, and sometimes genocide.

Though colonialism was repudiated and most colonies achieved independence, the circumstances of indigenous peoples has not improved in countries where newly independent nations adopted the preexisting colonial system for dealing with indigenous peoples. In such nations, colonial patterns still exist. The paramount challenge to human rights in these nations, including our own, is to find just ways to protect the human, political, cultural, and property rights of their indigenous people.

Contemporary issues, including those of culture, can be understood against the backdrop of colonialism and the closely related need to strengthen laws to protect indigenous rights. For example, colonists invariably retained close cultural ties to their distant homelands and rarely adopted their indigenous neighbors' values, cultures, or ways of looking at Mother Earth. Instead, they imposed their cultures, languages, and religions upon tribal people through the use of missionaries, schools, soldiers, and governments.

In the mid-1800s, U.S. government policymakers used the "Vanishing Red Man" theory, which was advanced by anthropologists at the time, as justification for the forcible removal of Native American tribes and for taking their lands. The policy did not work; America's indigenous peoples did not "vanish" as predicted. Native American tribes are still here despite suffering great difficulties since the arrival of Europeans, including an enormous loss of life and land brought on by disease, warfare, and genocide. Nonetheless, diverse groups survived, thrived, and continue to be an important part of American society.

Today, Native Americans depend on domestic law to protect their remaining cultural integrity but often that law is weak and ill-suited for the task, and sometimes does not exist at all. For example, U.S. federal law fails to protect indigenous holy places, even though other nations throughout the world take on the responsibility of protecting sacred sites within their borders. Congress is aware of this loophole in religious liberty but does not remedy it. Other laws promote assimilation, like the "English only" laws that infringe upon the right of Native Americans to retain their indigenous languages.

Another example concerns indigenous property rights. The *very* purpose of colonialism was to provide riches, property, and resources for European coffers. To that end, a massive one-way transfer of property from indigenous to nonindigenous hands occurred in most colonies. This included land, natural resources, and personal property (called *artifacts* by anthropologists). Even dead bodies (called *specimens* or *archaeological resources* by anthropologists) were dug up and carried away. The appropriation has been extended to intellectual property: aboriginal plant and animal knowledge patented by corporations; tribal names, art, and symbols converted into trademarks; and religious beliefs and practices *borrowed* by members of the New Age movement. Even tribal identities have been taken by "wannabes" masquerading as Native Americans for personal, professional, or commercial gain. In beleaguered Native eyes, little else is left to take. Native legal efforts attempt to stem and reverse this one-way transfer of property and protect what little remains.

Through it all, Native American tribes have played an important role in the American political system. The U.S. Constitution describes the political relationships among the federal government, states, Native American tribes, and foreign nations. Hundreds of tribal governments comprise our political system as "domestic dependent nations." They exercise power over Native American reservations, provide for their tribal citizens, engage in economic development, and sometimes come into conflict with states over intergovernmental disputes. Many tribes own and manage vast tracts of tribal land, extensive water rights, and other natural resources. The United States holds legal title to this property in trust. As trustee, the United States exercises significant power over the lives of Native Americans and their communities; and it is responsible for their well-being. These "nations within nations" are not found on international maps and are invisible to many in our own country.

Prior to 1900, about five hundred treaties between Native American tribes and the United States were duly ratified by the Senate and signed into law by the president. Treaties contain hard-fought agreements that were earned on American battlefields and made between Native American tribes and the United States. They opened vast expanses of Native American land to white settlement, protected remaining Native property, and created the political relationships with the U.S. government that remain to this day. As President George H.W. Bush said during his inaugural address in 1989, "great nations like great men must keep their word." Though many treaties were broken, many promises are honored by the United States today and upheld by federal courts.

The history, heritage, and aspirations of Native Americans create many challenges today. Concern for tribal sovereignty, self-determination, and cultural survival are familiar among Native Americans. Their struggles to protect treaty rights (such as hunting, fishing, and gathering rights), achieve freedom of religion, and protect Mother Earth (including land, resources, and habitat) are commonplace challenges, and sometimes include the task of repatriating dead relatives from museums. Each year, Congress passes laws affecting vital Native interests and the Supreme Court decides crucial cases. The hardships that Native Americans have endured to keep their identity are little known to many Americans. From the times of Red Cloud, Seattle, and Chief Joseph, Native leaders have fought to achieve these freedoms for their people. These ideals even today motivate many Native American soldiers to fight for our country in distant lands, like Iraq and Afghanistan, with the hope that the principles fought for abroad will be granted to their relatives at home.

Today, vibrant Native American communities make significant contributions to our rich national heritage. Evidence of this can be found in the recently opened National Museum of the American Indian, in Washington, D.C. It is also found throughout the pages of *Native Peoples* magazine and other Native media. It fills the best galleries, museums, and auction houses. It can be seen in the art, dance, music, philosophy, religion, literature, and film made by Native Americans, which rank among the world's finest. Visitors crowd tribal casinos and other enterprises that dot Native American reservations in growing numbers. Tribal governments, courts, and agencies are more sophisticated than ever before. Native American-controlled schools and colleges are restoring the importance of culture, traditions, and elders in education, and instill Native pride in students. The determination to retain indigenous cultures can be seen through the resurgence of tribal language, culture, and religious ceremonial life.

Yet many old problems persist. Too many Native Americans are impoverished and in poor health; living at the very bottom of almost all socioeconomic indicators and often in violence-ridden communities where disease, such as AIDS, knows no racial or cultural boundaries. Some socioeconomic problems stem from the aftermath of colonization of Native lands, peoples, and resources, or from efforts to stamp out Native culture and religion. Others stem from prejudice and hostility against Native people that has long characterized race relations in the United States.

As our nation matures, we must reject, once and for all, harmful policies and notions of assimilation and ethnocentrism, and embrace cultural relativism in our relations with the Native peoples who comprise our diverse society. History teaches where racial stereotypes, myths, and fictions prevail, human rights violations soon follow. But social change comes slowly and ethnocentrism remains deeply rooted in mass media and other corners of society. To little avail, Native people have told Hollywood to stop stereotyping Native Americans, protested against harmful racial stereotypes used by groups like the "Redskin" football team, and requested appropriate coverage of Native issues by the mainstream media. Native life is far different than how it has been depicted in the movies and by school and professional mascots.

Regrettably, schools do not teach us about Native Americans; textbooks largely ignore the subject. Sidebar information is provided only when Pilgrims or other American heroes are discussed, but Native Americans mostly "disappear" after dining with Pilgrims, leaving students to wonder about their fate. As a result, the people who met Columbus, Coronado, Custer, and Lewis and Clark are still here, but remain a mystery to legislators, policymakers, and judges who decide vital Native interests. Those interests are too often overlooked, marginalized, or subordinated by the rest of society. The widespread lack of education and information is the most serious problem confronting America's Native people today.

CONTEMPORARY NATIVE AMERICAN ISSUES will help remedy the information gap and enable youth to better understand the issues mentioned above. We are fortunate to have comprehensive data compiled in this series for students. Armed with facts, this generation can address Native American challenges justly.

Walter R. Echo-Hawk
Boulder, Colorado
March 2005

Introduction

Paul Rosier

During the mid-1970s, I attended Swarthmore High School in suburban Philadelphia, Pennsylvania. There, I learned little about Native Americans other than that they had lived in teepees, hunted buffalo, and faced great hardships in adapting to modern life at the end of the nineteenth century. But I learned nothing about Native Americans' experiences in the twentieth century. And as a member of the Tomahawks, the high school football team, I was constantly reminded that Native Americans had been violent and had used primitive weapons like tomahawks. Movies and television shows reinforced these notions in my young and impressionable mind.

It is my experience from teaching Native American history at the university level that students in middle and high schools across the country, have not, with some exceptions, learned much more about Native Americans in the twentieth century than I did thirty years ago. Several years ago, one of my students asked me if Native Americans still live in tepees. He and many others like him continue to be presented with a limited and biased interpretation of Native Americans, largely from popular culture, especially sports, where professional teams, such as the Washington Redskins, and mascots, such as the University of Illinois' Chief Illiniwek, continue to portray Native Americans as historical objects, not as citizens of this nation and as members of distinct tribal communities.

In 1990, President George H.W. Bush approved a joint resolution of Congress that designated November National Indian Heritage Month, and over the following years similar proclamations were made by presidents William J. Clinton and George W. Bush. On November 1, 1997, President Clinton stated: "As we enter the next millennium we have an exciting opportunity to open a new era of understanding, cooperation, and respect among all of America's people. We must work together to tear down the walls of separation and mistrust and build a strong foundation for the future." In November 2001, President Bush echoed Clinton by saying, "I call on all Americans to learn more about the history and heritage of the Native peoples of this great land. Such actions reaffirm our appreciation and respect for their traditions and way of life and can help to preserve an important part of our culture for generations yet to come."

We still have work to do to further "understanding, cooperation, and respect among all of America's people" and to "learn more about the history and heritage of the Native peoples of this great land." The information presented in CONTEMPORARY NATIVE AMERICAN ISSUES is designed to address the challenges set forth by presidents Clinton and Bush, and debunk the inaccurate perceptions of Native Americans that stretches back to our nation's founding and continues today. For example, schoolchildren's first intellectual exposure to Native Americans may well be through the Declaration of Independence, which describes Native Americans as "merciless Indian savages, whose known rule of warfare is an undistinguished destruction of all ages, sexes, and conditions."

The series' authors are scholars who have studied and written about the issues that affect today's Native Americans. Each scholar committed to write for this series because they share my belief that educating our youth about Native Americans should begin earlier in our schools and that the subject matter should be presented accurately.

Outside the classroom, young students' first visual exposure to Native Americans likely comes from sporting contests or in popular culture. First impressions matter. C. Richard King, Associate Professor of Comparative Ethnic Studies at Washington State University, discusses this important issue in his volume, *Media Images and Representations*. King looks at how these early impressions of Native Americans persist in film and television, journalism, sports mascots, indigenous media, and the internet. But he also looks at how Native Americans themselves have protested these images and tried to create new ones that more accurately reflect their history, heritage, and contemporary attitudes.

In *Education and Language Restoration*, Jon Allan Reyhner examines the history of how Native Americans have been educated in boarding schools or mission schools to become assimilated into mainstream American society. Reyhner, Professor of Education at Northern Arizona University, considers how Native Americans have recently created educational systems to give students the opportunity to learn about their culture and to revitalize dormant languages. Like non-Native American students, Native students should invest time and energy in learning about Native American culture and history.

This educational process is important to help Native Americans deal with a myriad of social problems that affects many communities in our country. In their volume *Social Life and Issues*, Roe W. Bubar and Irene S. Vernon, professors at the Center for Applied Studies in American Ethnicity at Colorado State University, review the various social issues that Native Americans face, including health problems like AIDS and alcoholism. They also consider how Native American communities try to resolve these social and health crises by using traditional healing ceremonies and religious practices that are hundreds of years old.

One very important issue that has helped Native American communities heal is repatriation. Joe Edward Watkins, Associate Professor of Anthropology at the University of New Mexico, examines this significant matter in his volume, *Sacred Sites and Repatriation*. Repatriation involves the process of the government returning to individual tribes the remains of ancestors stolen from graves in the nineteenth century, as well as pots and ceremonial objects also taken from graves or stolen from reservations. Native Americans have fought for the return of objects and remains but also to protect sacred sites from being developed. Such places have religious or spiritual meaning and their protection is important to ensure continued practice of traditional ceremonies that allow Native Americans to address the social and health problems that Vernon and Bubar describe.

In *Political Issues*, Deborah Welch, the Director of the Public History Program and Associate Professor of History at Longwood University, writes about how Native Americans reclaimed political power and used it to strengthen their communities through legislation that promoted both repatriation and the protection of sacred sites, as well as their ability to practice their religion and traditions, which the federal government had prohibited into the 1970s. Native American tribal communities have fought for their sovereignty for decades. Sovereignty means that tribal governments set the rules and regulations for living within reservation boundaries. Federally recognized tribal groups maintain their own courts to prosecute crimes—with the exception of major crimes, that is, rape, arson, and murder. Native Americans living on their own reservations generally do not need to obey state regulations pertaining to hunting and fishing and do not pay state income or excise taxes, though they are responsible for paying federal income taxes.

Tribal governments also help to create economic opportunities for their people, the subject of Deborah Welch's second volume, *Economic Issues and Development*. In this book, Welch examines the ways in which Native Americans have tried to create employment in businesses, which include ranching, mining, golf resorts, and casinos. She also considers how Native Americans have tried to develop projects within the context of their environmental traditions. As with other elements of their lives, Native Americans try to use their tribal histories and ceremonies to confront the economic challenges of modern life; to prosper by being *both* Native and American, while ensuring the health of Mother Earth.

Limited coverage of Native American life in schools, newspapers, and broadcast media has helped to perpetuate Americans' stereotypical views of Native Americans as either wealthy from gambling or suffering from poverty and alcoholism. The real picture is not so easy to paint and involves more than 560 separate Native American nations within the United States, which includes 4.1 million people who identify themselves as solely or in part Native American. The goal of this series is to explore the many different dimensions of the complex world of today's Native Americans, who are divided by geography, politics, traditions, goals, and even by what they want to be called, Native American or American Indian. Most Native Americans, however, prefer to be identified by their tribal name, for example, Lakota (Sioux), Blackfeet, or Diné (Navajo). And yet Native Americans are some of the most patriotic Americans, in part because their ancestors and relatives have died fighting in the name of freedom, a freedom that has allowed them to be both Native and American. As U.S. Army Sergeant Leonard Gouge of the Oklahoma Muscogee Creek community put it shortly after the September 11 attacks, "By supporting the American way of life, I am preserving the Indian way of life."

Paul Rosier
Villanova, Pennsylvania
March 2005

1

Native American Social Issues in the Twenty-First Century

Grandfather,
Look at our brokenness.
We know that in all creation
Only the human family
Has strayed from the sacred way.
We know that we are the ones
Who are divided
And we are the ones
Who must come back together
To walk in the Sacred way.
Grandfather,
Sacred One,
Teach us love, compassion, honor
That we may heal the earth
And heal each other.
—Ojibway Prayer[1]

INTRODUCTION

As Native Americans enter the twenty-first century, much of their way of life has changed even as whole other segments of their culture and lifestyle have remained the same. It is within this complex structure of continuity and change that this book examines Native social issues and concerns, both in a contemporary context and in honoring traditional systems that have kept communities in balance. The following chapters will discuss both the historical background and current social challenges that Native people around the nation encounter.

Debates continue regarding just how long Native people have lived here. Many academics argue that they crossed the Bering Strait during the last Ice Age; however, Native Americans maintain that their origin stories place them here from time immemorial. How they came here and how long they have been here continues to be debated, but one can say with certainty that Native people have been here for a very long time, at least thirty thousand years. To survive for that length of time is not easy, because environments change dramatically. Continual adaptation is necessary for survival. To maintain life in an ever-changing environment, Native Americans relied on their ability to adapt, while maintaining strong cultural and traditional belief systems. These ways of survival and cultural maintenance were varied among the many groups of Native Americans. However, Native Americans have proven themselves resilient during upheaval and change. This book will introduce students to the varied social issues that Native Americans of this country have faced and the differing ways they have dealt with them.

Culture defines a way of life that includes beliefs, customs, and attitudes that distinguish one group of people from another, and is transmitted through language, story, material objects, ritual, institutions, and art from one generation to the next. For Native Americans, their culture remains distinct, yet similar to the past. Culture is also multidimensional and interconnected with each component or parts related to each other—economic, social, political, ideological, religious, etc. To understand the social issues facing Native Americans today, one must understand the multiple parts of Native culture. Basically, no part of culture is freestanding; each is responsive to and is affected by other parts, as it in turn affects them. As you will find in this book, the social issues that are mentioned are connected to various aspects of colonization, federal policy, and Native culture.

There are many social issues that Native Americans face in the twenty-first century, including major issues in the areas of law, sovereignty, economics, and education. This book, however, focuses only on contemporary social concerns in the areas of Native health, with a closer examination of HIV/AIDS, spirituality, religious traditions, continuance of culture and tribal reclamation of cultural resources, and family violence and child maltreatment.

Much has been written about Native people, and most people speak about "Indians" as if they are frozen in time. Even today, high school students conjure images of tepees, horses, braids, and turquoise when asked what they know about Indians. They may remember great male leaders of the past— Cochise, Geronimo, and Chief Joseph. Other students may be able to provide some information about Indian wars without knowing what the conflicts were about. In essence, most high school students today know very little about the contemporary life of Native Americans in the twenty-first century and even less about Native women and their children.

Social Life and Issues will fill in some of the misinformation and lack of knowledge about Native Americans today. This book, however, will not be exhaustive, given the complexities and diversity of Native Americans and their lives. American

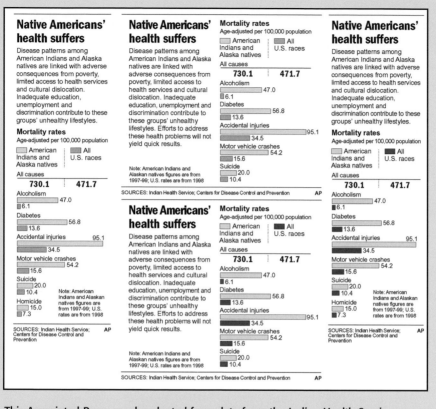

Native Americans' health suffers

Disease patterns among American Indians and Alaska natives are linked with adverse consequences from poverty, limited access to health services and cultural dislocation. Inadequate education, unemployment and discrimination contribute to these groups' unhealthy lifestyles.

Mortality rates
Age-adjusted per 100,000 population

American Indians and Alaska natives	All U.S. races

All causes
730.1   **471.7**

Alcoholism
47.0
6.1

Diabetes
56.8
13.6

Accidental injuries
95.1
34.5

Motor vehicle crashes
54.2
15.6

Suicide
20.0
10.4

Homicide
15.0
7.3

Note: American Indians and Alaskan natives figures are from 1997-99; U.S. rates are from 1998

SOURCES: Indian Health Service; Centers for Disease Control and Prevention   AP

Native Americans' health suffers

Disease patterns among American Indians and Alaska natives are linked with adverse consequences from poverty, limited access to health services and cultural dislocation. Inadequate education, unemployment and discrimination contribute to these groups' unhealthy lifestyles. Efforts to address these health problems will not yield quick results.

Note: American Indians and Alaskan natives figures are from 1997-99; U.S. rates are from 1998

SOURCES: Indian Health Service; Centers for Disease Control and Prevention   AP

Native Americans' health suffers

Disease patterns among American Indians and Alaska natives are linked with adverse consequences from poverty, limited access to health services and cultural dislocation. Inadequate education, unemployment and discrimination contribute to these groups' unhealthy lifestyles. Efforts to address these health problems will not yield quick results.

Mortality rates
Age-adjusted per 100,000 population

American Indians and Alaska natives	All U.S. races

All causes
730.1   **471.7**

Alcoholism
47.0
6.1

Diabetes
56.8
13.6

Accidental injuries
95.1
34.5

Motor vehicle crashes
54.2
15.6

Suicide
20.0
10.4

Note: American Indians and Alaskan natives figures are from 1997-99; U.S. rates are from 1998

SOURCES: Indian Health Service; Centers for Disease Control and Prevention   AP

Mortality rates
Age-adjusted per 100,000 population

American Indians and Alaska natives	All U.S. races

All causes
730.1   **471.7**

Alcoholism
47.0
6.1

Diabetes
56.8
13.6

Accidental injuries
95.1
34.5

Motor vehicle crashes
54.2
15.6

Suicide
20.0
10.4

Native Americans' health suffers

Disease patterns among American Indians and Alaska natives are linked with adverse consequences from poverty, limited access to health services and cultural dislocation. Inadequate education, unemployment and discrimination contribute to these groups' unhealthy lifestyles.

Mortality rates
Age-adjusted per 100,000 population

American Indians and Alaska natives	All U.S. races

All causes
730.1   **471.7**

Alcoholism
47.0
6.1

Diabetes
56.8
13.6

Accidental injuries
95.1
34.5

Motor vehicle crashes
54.2
15.6

Suicide
20.0
10.4

Homicide
15.0
7.3

Note: American Indians and Alaskan natives figures are from 1997-99; U.S. rates are from 1998

SOURCES: Indian Health Service; Centers for Disease Control and Prevention   AP

This Associated Press graph, adapted from data from the Indian Health Service, shows Native American mortality rates in 1998. Accidental injuries, diabetes, and motor vehicle crashes were the three leading causes of death among Native Americans.

Indians belonged to hundreds, perhaps as many as thousands, of different cultures. In the United States today, there are 562 tribes, including 230 villages in Alaska.

This book will ask several questions about a number of social issues. First, what is the health condition of Native Americans today and how has it changed over the years? What new diseases are they confronted with? What is the condition of tribal women and children? How has Native spirituality changed and why has it changed? What are the contemporary cultural resource issues facing Native Americans?

The challenges faced by Native Americans today are encountered in innovative ways that are based on tribal philosophies and ideas, and modern American ways. Students need to understand the complexities and richness of Native American lives and how their past remains a vital part of their future. In the words of former Cherokee chief Wilma Mankiller, "Crisis changes people and turns ordinary people into wiser or more responsible ones."

The essence of this book can be concluded with the words of the Onondaga faithkeeper Oren Lyons, who describes the importance of cultural maintenance even in the twenty-first century:

> In our way of life, in our government, with every decision we make, we always keep in mind the Seventh Generation to come. It's our job to see that the people coming ahead, the generations still unborn, have a world no worse than ours—and hopefully better. We walk upon Mother Earth and we always plant our feet carefully because we know the faces of our future generations are looking up at us from beneath the ground. We never forget them.[2]

2

Native American Health

·◇·◇·◇·

I didn't allow people to have more than one problem . . .
and when I walked away, I didn't feel I'd done a very good job;
I didn't give the best care I could, I didn't speak the language,
I didn't have the best facilities, and I turned away people.
—Albuquerque Journal, 2001

THE DISPARITY IN HEALTH CARE

The above words of Senate Majority Leader Bill Frist (R-TN) speak to one of the most pressing social issues facing Native Americans: "on average, African Americans and American Indians/Alaska Natives have higher overall rates of death than any other racial or ethnic group. American Indians/Alaska Natives, African Americans, and Hispanics are more likely to report poor health. One of the most sensitive indicators of health and well-being of populations is infant mortality rates, which are significantly higher in African Americans, American Indians, and Alaska Natives."[3] The health disparity gap found among Native Americans has a very long history and begins prior to colonization.

History

Before the arrival of Europeans, Native Americans governed themselves and determined their own health needs. Tribes had a variety of people who focused on various health needs. Tribal healers varied from tribe to tribe, were either male or female, and had a variety of skills. Some specialized in medicinal herbs, others conducted healing ceremonies, and some did both. At times the healing was done communally. The ways in which tribes chose to cure their sick were placed in the hands of those with the knowledge to heal. These people were sanctioned and approved by the tribe to deal with sickness and healing. Very early in the history of the exploration of the Americas, Christopher Columbus, as well as Dutch and French explorers and writers, commented on the well-formed and healthy bodies of Native Americans. This sense of strength and health began to deteriorate early with the onslaught of diseases that Columbus and others brought with them.

Health is one of the most critical social issues facing Native Americans today. Since colonization by European explorers and settlers, Native peoples have died in large numbers. By conservative numbers it is believed that there were 5+ million Native Americans living in the United States at the time of European contact. In the 1900s, the Native population dropped to its lowest point of 250,000.[4] Population decline was due primarily to disease; the Native people had no immunity. The diseases, themselves lethal, ran rampant when combined with grossly inadequate health care for the Native Americans and the lack of access to medical care for the Native people who contracted the new diseases. All these factors contributed to their demise. The poor health conditions of Native people was noted with the publication of the government-subsidized Meriam Report in 1928.

The Meriam Report

The Meriam Report found that during the 1800s, a time of great Native versus Anglo-European conflict, the U.S. Army took steps to curb infectious diseases, mainly to protect its soldiers. The first congressional appropriation for Indian health care was in 1832 and it was for the purchase and administration of the smallpox vaccine.[5] Civilian control over Indian health occurred in 1849 when the Bureau of Indian Affairs (BIA) was transferred from the War Department to the Department of the Interior. By 1880, there was a meager group of seventy-seven physicians serving the entire Native population in the United States.[6] At the close of the nineteenth century, Indian health funding continued to be insufficient, particularly because the U.S. government was not interested in providing health care to people they viewed as the enemy. It was not until the 1910s that Congress began to give money to the Bureau of Indian Affairs for medical assistance.[7]

The Meriam Report noted that virtually every activity assumed by the U.S. government for the promotion of Indian health was below a reasonable standard. In response to this report, Native health improved slightly with the increase of nurses, salaries for health service personnel, and hospital facilities. Provision of health care to Native Americans in the United States originates from treaties and is a part of the Unites States' trust responsibility to tribes. Although there was modest improvement in Native mortality rates, by the 1930s, Native mortality was still 50 percent higher than that of whites.[8] The number one killer of the time was tuberculosis.

Limited Improvements in Health Care

Improvement in health for Native Americans came about gradually for a number of reasons; mainly dealing with the economic, social, and political conditions surrounding Native communities. Slight improvements reappeared again in 1955 when the responsibility of Indian health moved from the BIA to the U.S. Department of Health, Education and Welfare. With this restructuring came an increase in the accessibility and availability of health services for Native populations but problems of access to health care continued to plague both urban and reservation communities.

More positive outcomes in health were achieved with the passage of the Indian Self-Determination and Education Assistance Act of 1975 (Public Law 93-638) and the Indian Health Care Improvement Act of 1976. With the passage of these acts came the federal Indian policy of self-determination, which is still the policy in place today. As a result, these acts encouraged, allowed, and funded Indian health programs run by Native people. The Indian Health Care Improvement Act was amended in 1988 and 1992 to further assist in the development of health programs for both urban and reservation communities. These acts supported and enhanced Native sovereignty, promoting self-determination and the implementation of PL 93-638 contracts, which enabled tribes to determine their own health needs and care. Even though many tribes have taken responsibility for administering their own health care, funding remains very inadequate for tribes already experiencing budget challenges. It is estimated that the shortfall to support contract costs and existing contracts is $150 million.[9]

Although life expectancy for Native men is now 69.4 years and 77.6 for Native women, these numbers reflect a current life expectancy that is still considerably lower (approximately six years less) than for all other races.[10] Native people continue to experience a number of health disparities and problems that occur more frequently than in other racial/ethnic groups within the United States. In the past forty years, Native health has improved but Native Americans continue to experience a number of major health issues. From 1940 to 1995, the average life expectancy for Native Americans increased 39 percent from approximately fifty-one years of age in 1940 to seventy-one years of age in 1995.[11] Old illnesses, such as tuberculosis and influenza, are being addressed but new diseases associated with poverty and harmful lifestyles affect the lives of many Native Americans today.

Native Americans in the twenty-first century continue to experience significant disparities in health status compared with the general population within the United States and there is a serious call to close the gap. Many factors have been identified as contributing to these disparities, including, but not limited to poverty, access to health care, years of neglect, diminishing resources for disease prevention, long-standing social and cultural disruptions, and a widening gap in health-care spending that forces rationing of health care. The gap in health-care spending is especially significant when the annual per-capita spending for Indian health is less than half the per-capita spending for the nation—$1,430 compared to $3,766.[12] This gap in health care results in delayed treatment or diagnosis, compelling patients to accept cheaper and less-effective treatment interventions, omission of treatment, or denial of services. Lack of adequate funding includes health-care delivery systems, which has affected the ability of the Indian health program to recruit and hire staff, to commit to long-range health planning to target resources for prevention and research, and to ensure culturally appropriate health care.

As a result of treaty promises, legislation, legal decisions, and a historical relationship with Indian tribes, the federal government has an ongoing trust responsibility to protect tribal lands, self-governance, and provide social services to Native Americans within the United States. Throughout U.S. history the federal government has not adequately met its trust responsibility to provide health care, education, and other bargained for trust responsibilities. Early land grants from Native Americans to the U.S. government were meant to grant land in perpetuity to non-Native Americans in

exchange for promises by the federal government to provide
health care, education, and other social programs for Native
peoples. However, the U.S. Commission on Civil Rights published a report in July 2003 that indicates that funding for services to Native Americans for health care, education, and law
enforcement is disproportionately lower than federal funding
for services to other populations within the United States. Of
particular note is that funding for Native American health care
is 50 percent lower than health care funding provided for pris-
oners or Medicaid recipients.[13] The average American secures
60 percent more for health care annually than Native
Americans.[14] That same federal trust responsibility to provide
health care applies to urban-based and reservation-based
Native populations. As a result of inadequate funding, there has
been a significant increase in the urban Native population,
because many people have opted to relocate to urban areas in
search of work, education, and a better quality of life. In 1990,
the urban Native population was 37.7 percent of the entire
Native population, while today the urban Native population
has grown to 60 percent.[15]

Native American Population in the United States

Today, U.S. Census data indicate that Native Americans comprise 2.5 million or almost 1 percent (0.9) of the U.S. population.[16] By 2050, it is estimated that Native Americans will reach
a population of more than 4.2 million. Native populations in
this country are younger than any other race/ethnicity by
almost eight years and half of the population is under twenty-
seven years of age.[17] There are 562 federally recognized tribes,
with the highest percentages of Native Americans located in
Alaska, New Mexico, Oklahoma, South Dakota, Montana,
Arizona, and California.[18] Sixty percent of the Native population within the United States lives in urban areas and the
remaining Native population is located on reservations, villages,
pueblos, colonies, rancherias, and other homeland areas.[19]

Leading Causes of Death among Native Americans

As the United States heads into the twenty-first century, there are four leading causes of death for Native Americans: diseases of the heart, malignant neoplasm (cancer), accidents, and diabetes.[20] Cardiovascular disease, or diseases of the heart, was not a major health problem for Native Americans in the United States until the late twentieth century. While cardiovascular disease is the leading cause of death for Natives, it is the fifth-leading cause of death for Alaska Natives.[21] The prevalence of cardiovascular disease is found to be increasing and there are a number of factors that place Native Americans at greater risk. They include high rates of smoking, high blood pressure, high cholesterol, diabetes, physical inactivity, and obesity. [22] Heart disease has also become a major source of disability, which has increased hospitalizations and inpatient and outpatient procedures, and resulted in an increase in Indian Health Services (IHS) spending and in Tribal Contract Health Service funds. This has placed a further burden on the cost of Native health care, which results in further health disparities.

Cancer

The second-leading cause of death for all Native Americans is cancer and it is also the leading cause of death among Alaska Native Americans.[23] Cancer rates for Natives vary significantly by region. Alaska and the Northern Plains populations have the highest rates.[24] It is important to note that significant numbers of Alaska Natives live in some of the most geographically remote communities and live a subsistence lifestyle in which they rely upon marine mammals, fish, birds, and animals that live migratory lifestyles. The most common cancers occurring in these two regions are cancer of the lung, colorectum, liver, stomach, and gallbladder.[25] In tribal communities of the Southwest, the lung cancer rate was four times lower than the occurrence among all racial/ethnic groups combined. According to the Centers for Disease Control and Prevention

(CDC), colorectal cancer is the second-most common cancer and the rates of this cancer also vary by tribal region. The Northern Plains and Alaska have the highest occurrence, whereas the Southwest has the lowest. Rates of lung cancer, which has been linked to smoking and cigarette use among Native populations, is higher than in white populations for both women and men. Some of the possible explanations for the higher incidence of smoking among Native Americans identified by the CDC may include lower educational and income levels, traditional use of tobacco, and concurrent alcohol use.[26]

Native women have a lower occurrence of breast cancer than other women in the United States. However, breast cancer is still a serious condition among Native women. Prevention, such as breast cancer self-exams and screening, remains a challenge in communities for Native women, whereas these types of prevention appear to be more commonplace in non-Native communities throughout the United States. Up until 1990, breast cancer screening was largely not available in tribal communities. Prevention programs that discourage smoking, and promote screening of colorectural and breast cancer should be increased and could have an impact on lowering cancer rates, especially in Alaska and the Northern Plains region.[27]

The National Indian Health Board (NIHB), whose vision is to advocate on behalf of tribes and Native people, has the single goal of promoting quality health care for Native Americans. Since its inception in 1972, the NIHB advocates on behalf of all federally recognized tribes in the development of a National Indian Health policy and also monitors federal and state legislations and works in collaboration with other health-care agencies. The NIHB also conducts research, program assessment and development, conference planning and training, and technical assistance to tribes, area health boards, tribal organizations, federal agencies, and private foundations. On their Web site (*http://www.nihb.org/*) are links and updated notices on a variety of health issues. The NIHB has also partnered with the Native

American Cancer Survivors' Support Network, which helps improve survival from breast cancer and the quality of life after diagnosis for Native patients and their families. They have also joined the Native C.I.R.C.L.E., a resource center that provides cancer-related materials to health-care professionals and others involved in education, care, and treatment of Native Americans.

Accidents

The third-leading cause of death among Native Americans and the leading cause for Native Americans ages one to forty-four years are unintentional injuries.[28] Alcohol and drug use, geographically isolated communities, underfunded federal initiatives, and a resultant lack of tribal infrastructure to address these challenges may all unintentionally contribute to the higher accident rates for Native children and adults. Because this is a health area that could be addressed with specific educational programs and interventions, it is worth a full discussion. Native death rates for unintentional injuries and motor vehicle crashes are 1.7 to 2 times higher than the rate for all other racial groups in the United States. Native Americans die in motor-vehicle-related deaths two to three times the rate of other Americans. Other injury-related deaths are caused by suicide, pedestrian-related deaths, drowning, fire, and burn-related deaths. The five leading causes of injury death are traffic-related (43 percent); homicide/suicide-related (33 percent); poisoning-related (6 percent); drowning-related (6 percent); and burns, falls, or other related (12 percent). There are differences by region and gender for both chronic disease and injury among Native Americans. A CDC telephone survey conducted from 1995 to 1998 indicated that in the Northern Plains, 54 percent of Native Americans were not wearing seat belts while driving or riding in a car, compared to 19 percent on the Pacific Coast. Native men (39.7 percent) were also at higher risk than women (30.5 percent) for not wearing a seat belt when driving or riding in a car.[29] Tribal educational campaigns targeting seat-belt use are largely being funded by the National Highway Traffic Safety Administration and Federal Highway Administration. Training, technology transfer, and education support are provided via the four regionally designated Tribal Technical Assistance Programs funded by the Federal Highway Administration and Bureau of Indian Affairs. There have been a number of successful tribal interventions and campaigns that have included enforcement strategies, enactment of laws or policies, education and awareness campaigns, and engineering and technology improvements.

Yakama Nation Occupant Protection Coalition

The Confederated Tribes and Bands of the Yakima Nation are made up of fourteen tribes and bands, most of whom live on a 1,377,034-acre reservation in south-central Washington State. The Yakama tribe has traditionally held the health and well-being of its people in high regard; operating the White Swan Health Clinic, a maternal child health center, and various health and social services, including programs that address alcoholism, nutrition, and the concerns of women and children.

In 2000, the Yakama Nation Occupant Protection Coalition was formed to gather information on seat-belt laws. Based on information presented to the tribal council, a seat-belt law was passed—by a vote of 10 to 0—and an education campaign was implemented for one year to inform the tribal community. The coalition sponsored child safety seat installation clinics, public service announcements on the tribal radio station, and an educational campaign that included posters, signs, and billboards on Yakama Nation roads. In addition, the Yakamas decided that half of the money collected from fines received from offenders would be used to purchase child safety seats that would go to those individuals who take part in the Maternal Child Health Program. The tribal council provides one verbal warning, one written warning, and then fines offenders $47 if children are not safely restrained.*

* For more information, please visit *http://www.nhtsa.dot.gov/PEOPLE/outreach/safedige/ Fall2001/F01_06W_INDIAN.html*

Smoking is more prevalent in Native populations located in the Northern Plains (45 percent) than in the Southwest (22 percent).[30] In most non-Native communities, multiple strategies have been implemented as prevention initiatives targeting both seat-belt use and smoking. Laws have been passed on seat-belt use, tickets are issued for non-use, child safety seats are mandatory for young children, national media campaigns have encouraged the use of seat belts, and in some situations criminal charges can be filed for noncompliance when children die because they weren't wearing seat belts or child restraint seats. In non-Native communities, smoking ordinances are becoming more commonplace and in some communities smoking is not allowed in any public place. Education campaigns about secondhand smoke are also commonplace in non-Native communities, where smoking ads are no longer televised, and smoking among adults has become a social stigma. Most Native communities do not have seat-belt laws, child-restraint seat laws, or smoking ordinances. Because law enforcement (tribal and federal) in tribal communities is underfunded and understaffed, effective and consistent enforcement of seat belt laws would present additional financial and infrastructure challenges for tribal communities.

Lastly, in examining the issue of high accident rates for Native Americans it is important to include a discussion on the role that alcohol plays in relation to accident rates. According to University of New Mexico sociology professor Philip May, drinking style may be the most sensible explanation for the differences in motor-vehicle deaths of Native Americans versus non-Native Americans when alcohol is involved.[31] Fatal motor-vehicle crashes of Native Americans in the Southwest, particularly in New Mexico, tend to be different than non-Native fatal motor-vehicle crashes.[32] Native Americans had a higher percentage of single-vehicle and pedestrian crash victims than non-Native Americans. Native Americans regardless of age, sex, or role in the crash tended to have a higher blood-alcohol rate than non-Native Americans.

Those highest at risk for alcoholism within the Native population tended to be involved in these types of crashes.[33] It should be noted that the use and occurrence of alcohol in Native communities is complex, surrounded in myth, and will be addressed in a subsequent section.

Sadly, preventable injuries for children account for almost 75 percent of all accident-related deaths of Native Americans age 1 to 29 years, compared to 64 percent nationwide from 1992 to 1996. Injury rates vary significantly depending on the region of the country. Children in Alaska and the Dakotas have an increased risk of fire-related and suicide deaths at five to seven times the rate for all children and youth. Suicide rates among Native youth are a critical concern in many tribal communities. Homicide rates for Native Americans are twice the national rate and suicide rates are 1.5 times higher in the Native population. The second- and third-leading cause of death in 1990 to 1992 for Native males between the ages of 10 and 34 was homicide and suicide. Homicide and suicide fluctuated during these years. During this same time period for Native women between the ages of 15 and 34, homicide was the third-leading cause of death. Today, suicide is the eighth-leading cause of death for Native Americans.[34]

Rates of Native children who are involved in motor-vehicle-related deaths are almost twice the rate for white children. In the Billings, Navajo, and Aberdeen Indian Health Service Areas, motor-vehicle-related deaths were more than three times the rate for all children in the United States. Tribal communities as well as federal agencies are working to develop more effective prevention programs that address injury and accidents among Native youth. Prevention and general health initiatives are simply underfunded and inadequate in tribal communities. Child deaths related to drowning are a critical concern in many remote Alaska Native communities where water temperatures and river currents present significant hazards to children.[35] One community in Alaska is promoting float-coats and other flotation devices designed to prevent drowning. Other tribal communities have focused on decreasing the number of motor-vehicle-related deaths with a variety of educational campaigns. As discussed earlier, national funding for four regional Tribal Technology Assistance Programs was created to support the tribal infrastructure to promote tribal transportation programs and departments and bridge the technology gap many tribal communities are experiencing with limited funds and resources. Aha Bruce from the Turtle Mountain Band of Chippewa sums up these initiatives, "Selling a safe communities concept was easy because of our extended family philosophy. As Native people, we all look out for each other, whether related by blood or not. When someone is killed or injured, we all mourn."

Alcohol and substance abuse remain serious health concerns for Native peoples. At the same time, it is important to note that the use of alcohol in particular by Native people has been surrounded in misinformation for years and remains an educational challenge. Perhaps the most pervasive misinformation is the idea that Native Americans can't physically "hold their alcohol" because of some biophysical weakness. This phenomenon is commonly referred to as the "firewater" myth and is still a pervasive view held by many, including Native Americans. There is no support in the research for this premise and studies have concluded that alcohol metabolism and alcohol genetics are attributed to individuals and that there is more variation within subgroups than there is between ethnic groups.[36] More recent genetic research has shown that some Native Americans are more susceptible than others and that this susceptibility is not unique to Native Americans but instead is transmitted within families from generation to generation.

Prior to colonization, there were tribes that used fermented or distilled beverages. However, this number is small: only a few tribes out of hundreds historically partook in these beverages.

The Apaches and Tohono O'Odhams in the Southwest had access to and used these types of beverages for various purposes. What we have learned from history is that Native Americans initially turned down opportunities to use alcohol with non-Native Americans socially. Native Americans didn't like the effects of alcohol. Over time and with repeated introduction of alcohol by non-Native Americans, alcohol became a part of the trade relationship. Introduction of alcohol during trade negotiations could have weighed in the favor of traders because Native Americans didn't have experience drinking alcohol.[37] It is important to examine the social indoctrination around alcohol use for ethnic communities in order to understand how alcohol use is normalized. Native Americans did not have the same community modeling on alcohol use as Europeans and as a result initial alcohol use often resulted in unpredictable behavior, which frightened Europeans, reinforcing well-established stereotypes of Native Americans as "wild savages."

Native populations tend to have more people who abstain altogether from drinking than the general population. Interestingly, this is largely unknown among the general population. There have been efforts throughout reservation-based and urban-based communities to address drug and alcohol use. And while the Native population does have more "problem" drinking than the general population within the United States, per-capita drinking styles may be more important than prevalence in discussing the occurrence of alcohol use among Native Americans.[38] In 1968, F.N. Ferguson identified two primary drinking styles found in Native populations: the recreational drinker and the anxiety drinker.[39] The recreational or social drinker is younger and will typically drink with friends during social gatherings, weekends, or parties that may continue all night or all weekend. Philip May describes what is characteristic of this style of drinking that is not characteristic of non-Native Americans—the duration, speed, and quantity of

Diabetes is currently the fourth-leading cause of death among Native Americans and according to the Centers for Disease Control (CDC), they are 2.6 times more likely to develop diabetes than other race/ethnicities within the United States. Pictured here is Norm Underbaggage, who is waiting to receive his dialysis treatment in the Porcupine Clinic on the Pine Ridge Reservation in South Dakota.

alcohol consumed. This type of recreational drinking is often reinforced by social norms or expectations and intoxication may even be encouraged.[40] A number of researchers in this area note that young people who fall into this type of drinking pattern tend to quit drinking in this manner as they get older (30 to 35) and many chose to abstain altogether later in life.[41] The Native population as a whole is a considerably younger population than the general population of the United States and this may contribute to the prevalence of recreational drinking within tribal communities.[42]

Alcohol-related deaths often have a connection to the age of Native populations, which is much younger than the general population, and young people tend to have higher death rates due to alcohol-related accidents in general. In addition, the recreational-type drinkers are more likely to be found in this group of accident-related fatalities when alcohol is involved in accidents. Native communities tend to be geographically isolated and alcohol-related accidents are higher in these environments due to poor road conditions and lack of seat-belt use.[43]

Unlike the recreational drinker, the anxiety drinker tends to be older, drinks alone, drinks on a continuous basis, and has a history of personal and family dysfunction. Anxiety drinkers tend to have significant health challenges and often die from alcohol-related effects. And while individuals who fall into this category are clearly a minority of the Native population, they tend to be visible because many are without cars and are often on the street or hitchhiking.[44]

Diabetes

For the past forty years, diabetes—the fourth-leading cause of death among Native Americans—has continued to be identified as a major health concern among Native Americans in the United States. Diabetes impacts Native Americans disproportionately compared with other racial/ethnic groups and has been on the rise over the past sixteen years.[45] Native Americans are almost three times as likely to have diabetes as those among the general population. There are also indications in recent research that rates of diabetes are higher and increasing among the Native youth population. The Pima Indians of Arizona have the highest rate of diabetes in the world.[46] According to the CDC, Native Americans are 2.6 times more likely to develop diabetes than other race/ethnicities within the country.[47] One of the primary challenges with diabetes is the other complications associated with the disease, such as blindness, lower extremity amputations, kidney failure, and cardiovascular disease.[48] Native Americans are three to four times more likely to experience an amputation due to diabetes than the general population.[49]

Like other diseases in tribal communities, diabetes rates

vary by region. In 1998, the Southwest had the highest incidence of diabetes at 34.9 per 1,000 among Native Americans
age 35 and younger. Changes in Native lifestyle, diet, and environment may contribute to increased diabetes rates in tribal
populations.[50] Educational campaigns are in place in a variety
of Native communities to increase prevention efforts. Some of
the more promising strategies for reducing the rate of diabetes
include: early screening, early treatment, eye and foot examina-
tions, and improved treatment of complications associated
with diabetes.

The Zuni Wellness Center in New Mexico is a well-known
national and international community-based program that
promotes wellness and health among the Zunis. Their work is
focused on getting more Zunis who are at risk for diabetes to
participate in exercise and health promotion activities. The
Zunis also have a hospital-based diabetes program that has

Defining Diabetes

Among Native Americans, diabetes is the fourth-leading cause of death.
According to the Centers for Disease Control (CDC) in Atlanta, Georgia, there
are two types of diabetes:

Type 1 diabetes was previously called insulin-dependent diabetes mellitus
(IDDM) or juvenile onset diabetes. Risk factors are less well defined for type
1 diabetes than for type 2 diabetes, but autoimmune, genetic, and environmental factors are involved in the development of this type of diabetes.

Type 2 diabetes was previously called non-insulin-dependent diabetes
mellitus (NIDDM) or adult-onset diabetes. Type 2 diabetes may account for
about 90 to 95 percent of all diagnosed cases of diabetes. Risk factors for type
2 diabetes include older age, obesity, family history of diabetes, prior history
of gestational diabetes, impaired glucose tolerance, physical inactivity, and
race-ethnicity. Native Americans are 2.6 times as likely to develop type 2 diabetes than non-Native Americans.*

* Information adapted from the Centers for Disease Control's website: http://www.cdc.gov/
  diabetes/faq/basics.html

been in existence for seventeen years and has partnered with the Zuni Wellness Center. The Zuni Diabetes Program engages in research and education.

There is also a special federal diabetes program that was implemented for tribes in 1997. The initial amount of the appropriation for this program has steadily increased from $30 million a year to the current amount of $150 million a year for 318 grant recipients. At first glance this appears to be adequate funding; however, it is estimated that it costs between $5,000 and $9,000 a year to treat and care for a person with diabetes. Given the overrepresentation of diabetes in the Native population it is estimated that it would actually cost $425 million to adequately fund care for Native Americans with diabetes. Therefore, it is important to emphasize how underfunded the special diabetes program is within the federal health-care system responsible for treating the Native population.[51]

Mortality Rates

Alarmingly, health disparities among Native people are reflected in an array of mortality and morbidity statistics, including diabetes. For example, data from 1994 to 1996 indicate the following causes of age-adjusted death rates for Native Americans, which are greater than for all U.S. races: 1) alcoholism—627 percent greater; 2) tuberculosis—533 percent greater; 3) diabetes mellitus—249 percent greater; 4) accidents—204 percent greater; 5) suicide—72 percent greater; 6) pneumonia and influenza—71 percent greater; and 7) homicide—63 percent greater.[52]

Poverty

Poverty continues to present major social problems as well as health risks for Native Americans in the twenty-first century. Native Americans rank at or nearly at the bottom in social, health, and economic indicators. Poverty has a disparative impact on ethnic and racially diverse populations, children, women, older people, people who live both in the South and the West, and foreign-born citizens. The national rate for poverty between 1999 and 2001 was 11.6 percent; however, for Native Americans the poverty rate is 24.5 percent: Nearly one in four Native Americans lives in poverty within the United States. Poverty rates are even higher for reservation-based Native Americans, where 40 percent of the entire Native population resides with a poverty rate of 31.2 percent, indicating that one in three reservation-based Native Americans lives in poverty. Native Americans are twice as likely as the general population to face hunger.[53]

Other secondary risks associated with poverty are homelessness and violence. In 1997, James F. Short argued that poverty left people more vulnerable to victimization. Closely related to poverty are the unemployment challenges pandemic to tribal communities. Because most reservation and homeland areas are located in economically barren areas, economic development and adequate employment remain serious concerns for Native Americans. Unemployment in reservation communities varies greatly across Native populations. The unemployment rate for Native Americans is 12.4 percent, which is twice the national average. Unemployment tends to run even higher for reservation communities. The average unemployment rate for reservation-based communities is 13.6 percent, with Pine Ridge and Rosebud, South Dakota, at 33 percent unemployment, and the Kickapoo Reservation in Texas experiencing a 70 percent unemployment rate.[54]

It is clear that improving Native Americans' health is critical to their survival. Michael Bird, a former president of the American Public Health Association, said: "We must maintain our commitment within our indigenous communities to be supportive of each other. Together, we are strong and capable. We are not the sum of our disparities. We will enter the broad arena as brothers and sisters on our way to building appositive health and greater visibility for all of us."[55]

3

Native Americans and HIV/AIDS

*We may not be perfect but we can make a conscious effort
to be part of an unhealthy or healthy sexual experience.
Our actions can be part of a solution to address the HIVAIDS
epidemic or part of the problem. These decisions are ours alone.*
—National Native American AIDS
Prevention Center

THE NEW SMALLPOX?

A major concern of many in the field of Native health is the possible encounter with dangerous and unknown diseases, such as smallpox. Smallpox was one of the major killers of Native people. In the sixteenth and seventeenth centuries, smallpox brought massive destruction, killing whole tribes. By the 1800s, smallpox no longer destroyed entire tribes but it still caused serious damage. For some tribes, at that time, mortality rates from smallpox ran between

55 and 90 percent. Smallpox incited massive demographic disaster among Native people who were highly vulnerable to this new disease. An additional consequence of the many deaths caused by smallpox was the loss of leaders, knowledge, and the old and traditional way of life. For these reasons AIDS is seen as the "New Smallpox" because of its possible destructive behavior. As Native Americans begin to confront this new deadly disease, several factors have been found to place them at risk and many Native Americans and agencies are rising to combat it.

The Impact of AIDS on Native Americans

The overall number of Native AIDS cases is reported to be less than 1 percent. However, the low number is viewed with great skepticism due to a number of reasons: racial misclassification; underreporting; poor reporting from various health clinics to states; inclusion of insufficient population numbers to formulate conclusions; regional limitations for data collection, which cannot be generalized to all of Indian Country; other tribal communities; and the omission of data for urban areas. For example, many Native Americans have been misclassified in terms of race/ethnicity on data collection forms, due to assumptions about names, skin color, residency, and even intentionally misleading self-reporting. The issue of poor reporting and ways to improve it are currently being addressed by the National Native American AIDS Prevention Center and other agencies so that the collection of accurate data is sufficient to set health priorities and develop innovative health programs for Native people. Changes in the reporting system can account for some of this increase and Native Americans are not allowing low statistical numbers to numb them into complacency, because many of them are at high risk for infection.

Although Native Americans carry less than 1 percent of the reported AIDS cases in the United States, their numbers continue to climb. It has been found that the remote, isolated

In 2001, then-U.S. Surgeon General David Satcher (shown here) called AIDS a ticking time bomb for Native peoples—HIV infection among Native Americans is now 1.5 times that of whites and increasing. This jump in the number of AIDS cases has led some Native peoples, such as the Navajos, to introduce public service announcements that will influence tribal members to get tested for sexually transmitted diseases.

nature of many reservations protected Native people from the disease for a time, and in many instances the only cases found on reservations were people who had been infected in urban areas who returned home to die. But, by 2001, the rise in cases resulted in Surgeon General David Satcher calling AIDS a ticking time bomb for Native peoples. Most Native Americans diagnosed with HIV/AIDS are living in metropolitan areas but migrate to and from urban areas to traditional homelands. Socially, Native people are integrally tied to their homelands and recognizing these ties is important to understand the potential paths of the spread of HIV/AIDS. More than half the Native population lives in cities but many, if not most, migrate back and forth for work, ceremonies, and to visit family and friends. This circular movement is a potential high-risk behavior, as it may expose rural partners to the disease. Others worry that infected individuals who do not know their status are unknowingly passing the disease on to others.

Factors Influencing the Spread of AIDS among Native Americans

The increase of reported HIV/AIDS cases among Native people can be attributed to a variety of factors, including biological, economic, and social cofactors, as well as high-risk behaviors such as alcohol and substance abuse. The factors may vary from Native community to Native community, but many, if not all, very likely exist in most areas.

Biological factors that may assist the spread of HIV/AIDS are numerous and may vary among the various risk groups. One of the most serious biological cofactors that impacts women, men, and adolescents, and increases the risk for HIV/AIDS, is sexually transmitted diseases (STDs). The presence of an STD indicates high-risk behavior because protection did not take place. This is of great concern to those Native communities whose STD rates are high. Some communities' STD rates range from three to ten times higher than the general population. People who have or have had an STD are two to five times more likely to contract HIV. There are specific concerns for Native women because there are more men with the disease than women and women are more vulnerable to HIV because it enters more easily into their system. Older women also have concerns that relate to premenopausal and postmenopausal conditions and changes in their bodies. In efforts to address the association between HIV/AIDS and STDs, the Indian Health Service is calling for more education about their intersection.

Poverty is another economic cofactor that may contribute to the advance of HIV/AIDS and it is believed to be the leading cofactor in the advancement of the global AIDS pandemic. It was not until recently that the Centers for Disease Control and

Prevention (CDC) decided to collect socioeconomic data on persons with HIV and AIDS in selected states. In the United States and the world, HIV has moved unobstructed through impoverished communities. As indicated in a recent news release from the U.S. Census report, in a three-year average (1997 to 1999), 25.9 percent of the Native populations live below the poverty line compared to 11.8 percent of all other races.[56] Even though it presents an almost insurmountable challenge, economic conditions are key factors that must be examined in prevention and intervention efforts to reduce HIV/AIDS. We know that when poverty is prevalent, health education, access to good health care, and proper medical treatment are low priorities that can significantly impact the prevention and treatment of HIV/AIDS.

Economic factors also have a powerful influence on social behavior. Empowerment and effective communication are critical in providing Native Americans the tools for condom negotiations. Poverty contributes to one's dependency and sense of powerlessness when they are the one who "brings home the bread." Poverty keeps many Native Americans at home and, sometimes keeps them in violent and abusive situations that are related to other high-risk behaviors such as substance abuse.

Drug use and poverty are also tied to social behaviors that govern sex and money. Native Americans who are drug users are struggling simply to survive. In this instance, an individual who is exchanging sex for drugs or sex for money has little power to negotiate condom use, placing themselves in severe danger for HIV infection. The drug-use lifestyle also places Native Americans at further risk through exposure to assault, rape, and infected needles.

With poverty comes a host of other concerns, such as poor health, poor diet, and related diseases that make Native people more vulnerable to HIV infection and to developing AIDS. Related diseases of poverty include both tuberculosis (TB) and diabetes. The deadly intersection between these diseases is that they are found in many tribal communities and they weaken the immune system, which needs to be strong to combat HIV/AIDS. Diabetes is a disease related to poor diet that makes Native people vulnerable to HIV infection. Poor diet also weakens the immune system, which is important in preventing the progression of HIV to AIDS. Native health professionals are challenged when they treat individuals co-infected with HIV and TB, because complications may occur when taking HIV drugs along with TB drugs. Individuals with both TB (inactive) and HIV have a 100 times greater risk of developing active TB than people who are infected with TB alone. The high rate of TB in Native communities has convinced the National Native American AIDS Prevention Center to test the majority of clients in their case management network prior to enrolling them in case management. The relationship between HIV and diseases such as diabetes and TB is increasingly a topic of concern to all health officials.

Native Americans have found that fighting the spread of HIV/AIDS among their people requires service providers to pay close attention to not only prevalent diseases but also to the social conditions as well, particularly homophobia. The acceptance, tolerance, and/or discrimination toward Two-Spirit (gay, lesbian, transgender, bisexual) tribal members may vary from place to place but in many Native communities the treatment of Two-Spirits reflects the attitude of the dominant society to marginalize diversity expressed via sexual orientation. To fight this treatment, many tribal communities are attempting to bring back the old ways of the acceptance and value of alternative genders. Some tribal communities had more than male and female genders and participated in a variety of sexual orientations known by several names, such as *winkte* (Lakota) and *nádleeh* (Navajo). Many Native Americans today who have alternative gender lifestyles consider themselves Two-Spirits, which is a word derived from the Algonquian language and refers to a human being with both masculine and feminine qualities that are simultaneously manifested in a variety of ways. When HIV/AIDS is associated with homosexuality, it can become hidden with devastating results. Those results vary from participating in risky behavior due to the lack of education, failure to seek medical treatment due to risk discovery, and spreading the disease knowingly or unknowingly, all of which result in increased infection rates. Therefore, Native communities are addressing the degree of homophobia within their own communities. The changing of community norms and attitudes is a difficult task.

Homophobia in some tribal communities has added to the migration of Two-Spirits to urban areas for medical assistance. The lack of HIV/AIDS education, prevention, and quality care on reservations has encouraged many Native Americans to migrate from reservation to urban areas. As mentioned previously, according to the 2000 U.S. Census, approximately half of all Native Americans live in urban areas. Although the U.S. government is obligated to provide health care to members of federally recognized tribes, access to this care has proven difficult for many urban Indians. In response, some HIV/AIDS-infected Native Americans must travel back to their reservation to access Indian Health Services because the urban Indian health centers are few and greatly underfunded.

Both on the reservation and in urban areas, Two-Spirits continue to face discrimination as both a Two-Spirit and Native individual. Despite some advances, discrimination against people living with HIV is still pervasive and affects virtually every aspect of life from employment to housing and access to basic medical care. Discrimination can also be found in the areas of employment, child custody and visitation, medical care, housing and shelters, and in drug and psychiatric treatment facilities. This places a tremendous amount of stress on individuals attempting to deal effectively with an illness.

Other social factors that assist in the spread of HIV/AIDS

among Native people are denial and mistrust. Denial that HIV/AIDS is a problem tends to be an issue in urban, rural, and reservation communities. Many Native Americans believe that it is a "gay man's disease" that has nothing to do with Native people. Tribal communities that ignore the realities of the situations can unintentionally create fear and mistrust and, therefore, can also be reluctant to obtain and provide information and services.

A legacy of colonization has been a major reason that Native people do not trust the federal government, public health officials, and the intentions of Western doctors. Sadly, this mistrust is well-founded and examples can be found in each of the tribal histories, all the way back to the "gifts" of blankets infected with smallpox, up to the sterilization abuses of Native women in the seventies. This mistrust also extends to the Indian Health Services, where issues of confidentiality have been questioned and the quality of care has been debated. And, although IHS facilities serve a large Native population, only a small portion of cases are diagnosed there. These are particularly important factors to consider for IHS offices located in small tight-knit communities where rumors and innuendo are common. Clearly, this history of distrust prohibits some from seeking diagnosis, assistance, and medical attention.

Finally, one of the most critical factors placing Native people at risk for HIV/AIDS is their behavior. Substance abuse is found in many Native communities and it places people at risk for contracting HIV/AIDS. It is true that substance and alcohol abuse is not the route of transmission for HIV, but it plays a very critical role in the AIDS epidemic. Under the influence of drugs or alcohol, protective behaviors are forgotten or ignored and judgment about high-risk behaviors becomes impaired. Native drug users are also placed at risk because their behaviors are usually tied to unemployment, poverty, and an unhealthy lifestyle.

In a reexamination of alcohol problems among Native communities, it was found in 2003 that much we know about alcohol use among Native Americans was anecdotal, stereotypical, and fueled by bias and what has been found is that "alcohol problems are not nearly as serious as some stereotypes may suggest"[57] and that differences are present among different Native communities. Although it may not be as serious a problem as previously thought, it remains a very important risk factor for contracting HIV/AIDS. Some Native Americans believe that the use of alcohol was the main factor that placed them at greatest risk for HIV, with many individuals reporting blacking out while drinking and later learning that they had unprotected sex with strangers or people they normally would not have chosen as a partner. Both substance and alcohol abuse interferes with the body's use of vitamins and minerals and it decreases white blood cells, as well, which are important in fighting infection.

The current situation facing Native people is frightening because many of their communities have all the risk cofactors that advance the world pandemic of AIDS. Factors such as poverty, discrimination, poor quality of and limited access to medical care and treatment could present Native people with a new epidemic.

Stopping the Spread of AIDS

In the work toward stopping the spread of HIV/AIDS, open and honest communication is vital. For Native Americans, though, it begins by breaking the silence and having open and frank discussions about sex and sexuality. However, given the history of trauma, some Native families are dysfunctional and under these circumstances lack communication across genders and between adults and adolescents about important health topics such as sexual activity, pregnancy, contraception, and sexually transmitted diseases. In addition, some Native youth have not been educated about HIV/AIDS, which has resulted from poor family communication. Open and effective communication must take place because a large number of youth are sexually active and HIV is increasing among this group. Many barriers to effective communication and appropriate HIV/AIDS prevention and care are internal to Native societies. One internal barrier is the inability of Native Americans to discuss sex, because it is a taboo subject. Developing appropriate HIV/AIDS prevention/intervention language is important and it will come from understanding specific Native community cultures and norms. AIDS agencies among the Navajos have been able to cross those boundaries knowing that although talking about sex is taboo, they must talk about it to keep their people safe.

Another challenge in the fight against AIDS in Native American communities includes gathering baseline information to obtain ideas about the HIV/AIDS movement and to document the progress of the community. Conducting research can also be problematic in Native communities because they have endured a long history of being studied and researched, often with little or no say in the design, implementation, evaluation, or interpretation of the data collected. Many Native communities have also lost faith in the research process when information about their community has been published without prior review, knowledge, or approval. Research projects conducted on reservations have gone through some changes in the twenty-first century and a number of tribes have either established their own internal review board for research projects or a committee that addresses tribal research concerns. Many tribes assert ownership over the research results and review any articles produced for publication.

Native Americans have also found that in the field of care and treatment there is a serious lack of communication among organizations and entities addressing the HIV/AIDS epidemic. In response, many tribal entities have moved to engage in collaborative partnerships. One of the most prominent Native agencies at the forefront of the fight against HIV/AIDS and collaboration is the National Native American AIDS Prevention Center (NNAAPC), located in Oakland, California.

NNAAPC

In an effort to curb the spread of HIV/AIDS, there are a number of Native HIV/AIDS organizations. One of the most well-known is the National Native American AIDS Prevention Center. NNAAPC is a nonprofit corporation founded in 1987 in response to the lack of Native health agencies engaged in the work of HIV/AIDS among Native peoples. In 1988, NNAAPC received its first funding award from the CDC. An important aspect of this organization is that it is governed by an all-Native board of directors that includes HIV-infected individuals, tribal officials, public health professionals, health-care providers, and substance abuse program administrators.

The mission of NNAAPC is to stop the spread of HIV and related diseases and improve the quality of life for members of Native communities infected and affected by HIV/AIDS. In sum, its purpose is to provide resources to Native communities and to support community efforts by providing education and information services, training and technical assistance, and offering case management and client advocacy services to Native Americans with HIV/AIDS. NNAAPC is not an AIDS service organization or service provider; instead its function is to assist Native communities in order to support their capacity to effectively deal with HIV/AIDS.

In providing capacity building technical assistance to Native communities and organizations, NNAAPC provides training for Native American organizations, agencies, and communities and develops and disseminates publications. Technical assistance includes targeted, individualized assistance to aid Native communities in developing successful HIV/AIDS prevention programs. NNAAPC also provides consultation on program development, needs assessments, and leadership development. Training is offered through annual and semi-annual regional workshops. NNAAPC also addresses specific needs of tribes and agencies and provides specialized training workshops. NNAAPC publications include a newsletter, *Two-Spirit Update*, and a journal, *Seasons*. Publications, statistics, AIDS resources, videos, conference information, and funding opportunities can be found on their Web site at *www.nnaapc.org.*

NNAAPC, which was created in response to the lack of services for urban Two-Spirit men, has expanded its work to include all subtarget populations, policy work, and publications. As the most well-known Native AIDS agency, it has met with tremendous success working in both urban and reservation communities, because of its dedication, hard work, and compassion, as well as its interagency, intertribal, intergovernmental coordination, and sharing of work and information. With the work of NNAAPC and other Native AIDS organizations, tribal communities are taking a lead in combating HIV/AIDS among Native Americans.

The BEAR Project

A more tribally specific agency that is working to empower and protect its community from HIV/AIDS is the BEAR Project, which is sponsored by the Northwest AIDS Education and Training Center at the University of Washington. The BEAR Project, which stands for Building Effective AIDS Response, equips teams of health professionals at tribal health-care clinics to provide up-to-date, culturally sensitive health care to Native Americans with HIV/AIDS. The project also seeks to educate community members. In increasing HIV awareness, education, and testing, BEAR has been involved in media campaigns and outreach activities. As of 2003, BEAR has conducted seven trainings at tribal clinics. Its teams include physicians, nurses, traditional healers, substance abuse counselors, behavioral health counselors, pharmacists, dieticians, and social workers.

One of their important community outreach tools has been the award-wining video, *Community Support Is Strong Medicine*. The video helps create discussion and stimulates learning at community meetings. In June 2002, BEAR hosted the first annual Traditional Healers Conference, which provided open dialogue about HIV and Native Americans that included both traditional healers and Western medical providers.

Indigenous People's Task Force

Another community-based organization providing critical AIDS services is the Indigenous People's Task Force in Minneapolis, Minnesota. An important component of this agency is their *Ogitchidag Gikinooamaagad* (warrior/teachers) peer education/theater program, which provides youth with comprehensive HIV/AIDS prevention curriculum, theater instruction, and traditional teachings. The Ogitchidag Gikinooamaagad Players are Native youth who have participated in this instruction and then use storytelling, drama, music, and dance to educate other youth and communities about HIV/AIDS. The task force provides other services that are specifically geared toward Native women and Two-Spirits, including a fourteen-unit permanent housing program for Native people living with AIDS and a case management that includes the participation of Native spiritual leaders.

What all these agencies have in common is the acknowledgement, respect, and use of culture in promoting Native health and healing. Paying close attention to culture is becoming more and more important for Native Americans for a number of reasons. The United States is already a diverse country that is becoming increasingly more diverse through immigration. The inclusion of culture is how people recognize and respond to diverse health-care initiatives, which is critical in the development of effective health care and well-being for Native peoples.

Raising Awareness through the Use of Culture

Culture can be defined in a number of ways, but generally it is the sum of attitudes, behaviors, customs, and beliefs of a people that is passed from one generation to the next. It includes thoughts, styles of communication, ways of interacting, and views of roles and relationships. Basically, culture informs people of the world around them and how to behave in families, organizations, and communities. The importance of culture is also included in prevention efforts. HIV prevention has been found to work best when it promotes change through individual and community empowerment strategies informed by holistic and community norms, beliefs, and values. Prevention efforts have failed when they have not been developed for the specific communities and individuals affected, and when the messages are incompatible with basic needs, values, and norms. Cultural differences must also be recognized within groups, especially among the Native population, which is the most diverse ethnic group within the United States.

At the core of traditionalism and Native sacredness is a worldview, often held by even the most urban acculturated Natives, of understanding and respect for the circle of life. In this worldview, people, earth, air, water, and animals are connected and there is acknowledgment of the need of all beings to maintain balance in the world. Within this circle are respect, obligation, and responsibility. Understanding the worldview of Native Americans will assist in knowing the importance of the community and all the people in it. An understanding of Native worldview is especially important in the development of educational prevention materials, and the inclusion of elders and other members of local communities in the preparation can produce more acceptable and effective materials. In understanding the diversity of Native worldview, it is critical for those working with Native Americans to acquire an increased knowledge and understanding base regarding specific tribal culture and traditions.

A unique part of Native culture can be found in the tribal community's social structure, which may take several forms, including extended families, clans, moieties, bands, societies, and patriarchal or matriarchal structures. Understanding these structures and the social relationships that are part of the structures can be important for a number of reasons. One of the reasons is that certain responsibilities and obligations may be part of an individual's place within the social structure. Two-Spirit men, for example, have spoken about their role and the importance of their role as the ones who also help take care of children. In addition, the social place of Native women and Two-Spirits in any given community may relate to their treatment or lack of access to it. These unique aspects of social structure are taken into consideration in prevention/intervention for it to have optimal effect.

A basic component of the social structure found among most tribal groups is the sense of unity and responsibility for the health of the community. In many tribal communities, dealing with sickness and wellness is not just an individual or family concern but a community concern. It is, therefore, important to include both the target population and the entire community in HIV/AIDS prevention, intervention, and care.

The Retention of Native Language

An aspect of Native cultural survival that speaks to its strength and endurance is the retention of Native languages. Although thousands of Native languages have been lost due to colonization, approximately 200 different languages are still spoken. Native languages are still an important cultural component of Native life, with more than 281,000 Native speakers in the United States.

The importance of language is that it guides the way a community looks at the world and recognizes people's place in it. Also embedded in language are generations of wisdom that carry cultural values, which help shape a person's self-awareness,

Native children gather around a storyteller on the Barona Indian Reservation near San Diego, California. Storytelling is an important way for adults to teach children about health and healing.

identity, and interpersonal relationships. Language strengths, an individual's identity, and self-esteem can all be critical in creating a barrier to HIV infection.

Understanding and utilizing traditional tribal languages in some prevention efforts and interventions is critical because through storytelling communities learn about health and healing. Traditional tribal stories and legends grounded in tribal language organize the world and lay out the individual and communal responsibilities and obligations. Stories teach one how to live in the world, how to behave, how to heal, and how to survive. Native communities that speak their own language have stories and legends that help unify people. Utilizing this local cultural knowledge is a must to effectively communicate with different groups of people.

Each community will also have a form of language that is acceptable, respectful, and appropriate in talking about sex. The language used to talk about sex in tribal communities is based on cultural norms that must be learned and incorporated in prevention and intervention materials. Community-based organizations and people within the tribal communities have the best capacity to create materials that are most appropriate and effective for their communities. This also ensures accuracy of translation.

Awareness of diversity of language must also take into consideration the language of substance abusers, gang members, women, youth, and elders. Language must be appropriate for age, gender, and behavior (for example, drug users). Effective HIV/AIDS messages speak the language of the target-group population, as well as the culture in which it is imbedded.

Awareness of and incorporation of aspects of culture should not be limited to the development of HIV/AIDS prevention, intervention, and care. It must also be used in the assessment of existing programs and services. Cultural perceptions can be expanded to include an outcome index that is Native in nature. For example, at a round table on Native youth, a tribal man stated that he would know that the youth were well when they "walked with their heads up and sang the old songs." Culture must be used in all aspects of Native HIV/AIDS efforts to receive the optimal result, which is to eliminate HIV/AIDS.

Finally, cultural understanding and cultural competency are critical in providing effective HIV/AIDS prevention and care in tribal communities. And, to achieve our goals, academics, researchers, grassroots workers, funding agencies, tribes, states, and the federal government must make the effort to understand the cultural norms present in the communities where they work. Many tribal communities and agencies are fully engaged in determining their own health and the incorporation of their own cultural norms. It is through the sense of community and survival that many Native Americans are responding to HIV/AIDS. And, through independent efforts combined with the efforts of individuals, tribes, organizations, states, government, health officials, and academics, it is clear that Native people will not die silently or quietly.

4

Violence against Native American Women and Children

The honor of the people lies in the moccasin tracks of the women.
Walk the good road. . .
Be dutiful, respectful and modest, my daughter.
And proud walking . . .
Be strong with the warm, strong heart of the earth.
No people goes down until their women are weak
and dishonored, or dead upon the ground.
Be strong and sing the strength of the Great Powers
within you, all around you.
—Village Wise Man, Sioux 1961

Other social health issues that have been impacted by the changes in traditional lifestyles, marginalization, underfunded initiatives, and federal policies, include domestic violence, sexual assault, and child abuse. Therefore, it is critical to consider the relationship colonization has to both historical trauma and violence against Native

Americans, and in particular violence against Native women and children. This chapter will begin with a discussion of colonization and will include an explanation of historical influences, as well as present-day factors that may contribute to domestic violence, sexual assault, and child abuse in tribal communities.

THE IMPACT OF COLONIZATION

Historical trauma and colonization resulted in sanctioning violence against Native people, deterioration of traditional support systems for Native women, adoption of the dominant culture's view of women resulting in economic deprivation, and impoverishment of tribal communities. These factors will be explored as they contribute to an understanding of the high rate of violence experienced by Native women. Understanding violence against Native women must begin with a foundation of the historical context of today's tribal communities. Initial colonization, subsequent federal Indian policy, and under-funded initiatives to keep tribal communities safe continue to impact tribal cultures and create conditions that promote violence.

Land Acquisition

Attempts to eradicate Indian nations began with land acquisition. Land acquisition has always been central to the domination of a foreign presence in this country. The legal fiction to create a basis for land title in North America was the doctrine of discovery. Under this doctrine, the sovereign discoverer could seize land already occupied by infidels to extend their Christian sovereignty over the land and the indigenous peoples who resided there. Colonial as well as European constructs of non-Christian indigenous peoples as infidels and therefore inferior, furthered the colonization of North America and shaped attitudes and subsequent federal government policy. Once the land was acquired, invading colonists continued to exploit Native peoples economically, politically, and socially.

The political autonomy today of Indian nations continues to be hamstrung by Congress' plenary (absolute) power and the slow yet continuous erosion of tribal sovereignty that continues in the federal and supreme courts.[58]

Colonization, which brought oppressive federal policy and genocidal initiatives, forced change. Relocation and assimilative federal policies resulted in the loss of traditional homelands and lifestyles, while also creating a dependency on the federal government, a loss of identity, and a loss of traditional cultural knowledge. In addition, it placed Native women at greater risk for violence, disrupted family life and parenting, and created loss of familiar and communal support systems. Disparate treatment of Native Americans resulted in what is known in Indian Country as "historical or intergenerational trauma." According to Bonnie Duran and Eduardo Duran, "Historical trauma or intergenerational trauma . . . is offered as a paradigm to explain, in part, the root or basis of the problems that have plagued Native Americans for many generations."[59] Although the idea of intergenerational trauma has long been known to healers and elders in Native communities, it is new to some researchers. Duran and Duran have pointed out that historical trauma is discussed in clinical studies throughout the literature pertaining to the study of Jewish Holocaust survivors. Intergenerational grief and historical trauma is the psychological residue from federal policies, which marginalized Native culture and employed violence as a weapon to force assimilation.[60]

Boarding Schools

One of the most pervasive examples, and one of the most destructive and genocidal federal Indian policies, was forced boarding school education for Native children. Beginning in 1869, and continuing for nearly one hundred years, Native children as young as five years of age were forcibly taken from their families and many never saw their home again until the

Boarding schools such as Carlisle Indian School in Pennsylvania were designed to indoctrinate Native Americans in the ways of Anglo-European society and to stamp out their traditional culture, family patterns, and communal behaviors. Shown here is a group of Sioux boys shortly after their arrival at Carlisle in 1879.

age of seventeen or eighteen.[61] By 1889, boarding school was made mandatory for all Native children ages five to twenty-one. The boarding school program was designed to eradicate traditional culture, family patterns, and communal behaviors.[62] As a result, many children were impacted by the institutional-ization of violence implemented in the schools and were largely unequipped to then deal with their own trauma later in life. Because this policy was in place for such a long time, the impact on families, clans, communities, and tribes cannot be over-stated.

Physical, spiritual, emotional, and sexual abuse were com-mon experiences for many Native children in boarding schools in the United States and in Canada.[63] Routine oppres-sive acts institutionalized in boarding school settings included ritualistic cutting of children's hair; the suppression of Native languages, religion, and culture; and physical, and/or emotional abuse of children who did not or would not comply. Many researchers and scholars maintain this deliberate attempt to suppress Native culture and force assimilation by violence impacts the Native psychological make-up even today.[64] Most families have mothers, fathers, aunts, uncles, or grandparents who attended boarding schools and it is not uncommon to hear about their experiences within the family. For some people boarding school offered good nutrition, warm clothes, and the promise of learning a trade during a time when many tribes were struggling economically. For others boarding school was a place where they lost their family, homeland, language, culture, and innocence. The Indian boarding school experience is still a recent memory for most—within a generation in the lives of many contemporary Native families. The boarding school experience reminds us that the European and Euro-American influence of culture, policies, gender politics, values, and laws greatly influenced indigenous populations throughout North America.

Domestic Violence

The incorporation of Euro-American gender politics and values into tribal life has clearly affected the presence of and tribal responses to domestic violence, sexual assault, and child abuse. In examining the problems Native women encounter in living violence-free, it has been argued that the destruction of traditional community responses to abuse has allowed violence to exist. Traditional tribal methods of violence interventions, which included banishment or ostracism, have been eliminated and are limited or less effective within the modern context with the incorporation in many tribal judicial systems of what was considered by some as a more acceptable Euro-American criminal justice system. There has been a revival of indigenous justice systems in a number of tribal communities throughout the country. However, indigenous justice systems have posed a number of challenges for women and children when attempts have been made to include domestic violence or child abuse cases within the context of family conferencing, mediation, or peace-making systems.

Throughout tribal communities, many Native people believe that the pain and suffering inflicted on Native Americans in the past has contributed to their suffering today. The colonization of Native Americans is an important aspect of understanding domestic violence because it resulted in the destruction of family and communal structures that protected both women and children. When Europeans arrived in North America, they brought with them foreign laws and ideas. European laws and social customs did not support women's rights. For example, British common law allowed wife-beating if a husband used a rod no thicker than his thumb, commonly referred to as the "rule of thumb." Prior to the rule of thumb, men were allowed to beat their wives with anything. Thus, physical abuse was not only a socially accepted part of family relations but was also legally sanctioned. Other European concepts were that women could not own land, had little legal control over their children, worked only in gender stereotyped jobs, were largely considered property, and did not participate in government.

European concepts influenced American colonial laws and were in great contrast to the status Native women held in many tribal societies. As Theda Perdue discusses in her book *Sifters*, women could own land, divorce their husbands, exercise control over children and resources, and participate in tribal government.[65] Furthermore, some Native communities, such as the Iroquois, were matriarchal, and Native women held significant status as clan mothers. Their political power included the ability to choose tribal leaders, as well as the power to remove them.[66] These matriarchal communities in the Northeast were a stark contrast to the more common patrilineal communities of the first European colonizers. In general, Native women were honored, held in great esteem, and mainly lived in egalitarian societies. Even when tribes implemented strict divisions of the sexes in work and social activities, there was still an acknowledgement of comparable worth, value, and honor across genders.[67] Theresa Halsey, a Hunkpapa Lakota from Wakpala, South Dakota, is a community activist who maintains that Native women have been the heart and soul of indigenous resistance to colonization and genocide since the first conflict with non-Natives.[68] Other tribal women emphasize the role Native women have historically held, and the protection provided them has changed considerably since colonization.[69]

Native Worldviews Govern Beliefs

It is important to also understand that Native families were not immune to violence prior to contact, but their worldviews governed their treatment of others. Native worldviews that consisted of honoring interdependent relationships, which in turn dictated the need for group survival, outweighed the hostility of individuals and disrupted the balance of relationships. The extent of domestic violence, sexual assault, and child abuse in precolonial tribal communities remains somewhat of a disputed issue. There are some who believe violence against Native women was not a community concern in precolonial times, while others acknowledge that gender-based dominance issues in some tribal communities did place women at greater risk for intimate partner violence. Yet many would agree violence was addressed quickly, sanctioned severely, and that some tribal communities would banish offenders, which resulted in their own demise because they were left without the protection and support of the tribe.[70] Many scholars would agree how Native women were treated and the roles they played in their tribal communities varied among the tribes in North America.[71] However, colonization and subsequent federal policy in Indian Country has resulted in greater oppression and less protection for Native women and their children. Historical and present-day trauma may put women as well as children more at risk for being victims of violence at the hands of both Native and non-Native offenders.

Violent Crime Rates among Women

Even as violent crime rates have fallen throughout the nation for most ethnicities, the same has not held true within Native communities. In the twenty-first century, Native Americans suffer the highest violent crime victimization rates in the nation—twice the rate for other Americans.[72] Of special concern is the violence against Native women and the rise of child abuse.[73] These both are serious problems by themselves and even more serious when combined, because it has been found that Native women at highest risk for domestic violence are also at risk for other health challenges. And women who report a current history of domestic violence may have been victims of abuse as children.[74]

Gender-based violence and trauma is emerging as one of the most serious health issues for Native women today. Violence against women or domestic violence is usually thought of as acts of violence between adult partners, whereas family violence is much broader and includes violence between adult partners, a parent against a child, caretakers or others against an elder, and violence between siblings. Violence is used in a broad sense and can include physical, emotional, or verbal violence. There is a serious lack of data and research concerning violence against Native women. In tribal communities today Native people in general are experiencing severe economic deprivation, high unemployment, and substance abuse and alcohol-related challenges. As with rural communities in general, and Native communities in particular, social isolation and economic hardship creates stress that may place Native

Americans at a higher risk for family violence.[75] It is the historical domination of Native peoples, oppressive federal policies, and continued underfunding of tribal initiatives that sets the stage for social isolation, economic hardship, poverty, and social challenges that have put tribal communities and their members at greater risk.

Rates of violence against women are higher for Native women than for any other women in the country. In fact, Native women experience a rate of violent crime 50 percent higher than that experienced by African American men.[76] U.S. Census estimates indicate that on reservations, households that do not have telephones—which can be an indication of both social isolation and economic deprivation—can have a rate of violence as high as 60 percent. Most of the data available on intimate partner or domestic violence in Native communities is not tribally specific, and given the great diversity of tribal populations it is difficult to get an accurate picture of violence against Native women. And perhaps most striking in the report is the race of offenders in intimate partner violence. Among Native women who are victims of intimate partner violence, 75 percent of the victimizations involve an offender of a different race. Within families, 25 percent of family victimizations involve an offender of a different race. Among violence victims of all races those rates are 11 percent and 5 percent, respectively. We now know Native women are victimized in intimate partner relationships more than other women and the offenders are most often non-Native men.[77]

Native women in Alaska experience violence at rates that far exceed both state and national averages. In the National Violence Against Women Survey, Native women were raped 15.9 percent of the time by an intimate partner. In 1998, Patricia Tjaden and Nancy Thoennes reported this incidence of rape by an intimate partner is significantly higher than for women of other ethnicities.[78] Nearly 75 percent of Native American and Alaska Native female homicide victims are killed by someone they know. And of that number approximately one-third are killed by a family member.[79] In evaluating treatment services for victims as well as their batterers, it is important to consider who the perpetrators are, where they are from, what criminal jurisdiction there is over these offenders in tribal communities, and how violence against Native women may be historically sanctioned and perhaps condoned by non-Native influences. At present, tribes cannot exercise criminal jurisdiction over non-Native Americans; only the state or federal governments exercise criminal jurisdiction over non-Native Americans in Indian Country. This causes serious challenges and concerns for the protection of Native women within their own tribal communities when a large percentage of the offenders are non-Native Americans and tribes do not have criminal jurisdiction over any non-Native Americans in Indian Country.

While intimate partner violence, sexual assault, and child abuse have been the subject of a plethora of recent studies in the United States, there is a paucity of research and accurate data on intimate partner or domestic violence in Native communities, and especially research directed to differences among tribes.

In the 1999 Bureau of Justice Statistics Report on American Indians and Crime, Native women suffered 7 rapes or sexual assaults per 1,000 compared to 3 per 1,000 among African Americans, 2 per 1,000 among white, and 1 per 1,0000 among Asian Americans. Native women experience significantly more rapes or sexual assaults than any other group of women in the United States.[80] In 1994, the Native American Women's Health Education Resource Center reported that based on a survey administered in South Dakota, 87 percent of Native females in twelfth grade reported having had sexual intercourse. What is particularly alarming about this figure is that 92 percent of the girls who reported having sexual intercourse also reported having been forced against their will to have sexual intercourse on a date. These South Dakota statistics reflect a national trend noted in the 1998 study, "Prevalence, Incidence, and Consequences of Violence against Women: Findings from the National Violence against Women Survey," which found that rape is a crime committed primarily against youth. What is important to note in this report is that Native women were more likely to report rape and physical assault than all other groups of women surveyed.[81] Most of the reports and national data available on the victimization of women and children is not necessarily tribal-specific and it is difficult to obtain an accurate picture on what is happening to Native women in individual tribal communities. In addition to obtaining tribal-specific data, it is also important to consider what factors may be contributing to violence against Native women and children.

Diversity Presents a Challenge

The diversity of Native American populations presents a challenge for both research and prevention. Native Americans are diverse in language, traditions, ceremonies, and customs, in both precolonial and postcolonial contexts. Tribes may be either patrilineal or matrilineal societies, and women's role and place in the community vary greatly. How gender dominance, historical practices/protections, and colonization are understood and impact Native women today is an area of controversy. Many would agree that colonization in tribal communities has introduced European notions of gender dominance and encouraged male privilege, male authority, male restrictiveness, and socioeconomic stress, all of which put women at greater risk for violence.[82]

Economic deprivation and the impoverishment of Native communities was commonplace in postcolonial America and were also important factors in changing gender relations. According to the National Center for Injury and Control, constant economic and subsistence deprivation likely were and are still risk factors for intimate partner violence among Native Americans. While violence against women is an issue for all classes, poverty remains a stressor that likely increases the possibility of violence.[83] In the 1999 Bureau of Justice Statistics Report on American Indians and Crime, Native Americans with incomes less than $10,000 a year have had the highest rate of violent victimization.[84] More recent research in 2004 has supported this and reaffirmed that poverty is a risk factor for violence against Native women.[85] Another factor that has been associated with the risk for violence against Native women and children has been the use of alcohol.

Alcohol and Violent Crimes

Violent crime in Indian Country is more likely to involve the use of alcohol if the offender is Native. Among violent crimes in Indian Country, 38 percent involve the use of alcohol by the offender, compared to 28 percent for all other groups. Offender alcohol use in violent crimes is higher and therefore different than in non-Native cases.[86] The use of alcohol by the victim has also become an area of concern for advocates in Indian Country. Many advocates say they are concerned when investigators learn that the victim had been drinking and later find out that those particular cases were not seriously investigated.

Not much has been studied on Native women and alcohol use and there is considerable difference in the amount of research conducted on Native men and alcohol use. In early studies on alcohol use in reservation populations, Native women abstained more than men and fewer women used alcohol than men.[87] In more recent studies, there are differences within and across tribes with respect to prevalence in populations of Native women and men. In some areas, women drink substantially less than men, and in other regions of the country women drink as much or nearly as much as men.[88] As discussed in chapter 2 on health, it is important to consider the impact that drinking styles have in understanding alcohol use in tribal communities. Despite the fact that women abstain more from drinking than men, those women who do drink to excess tend to have serious physical consequences as a result.[89] While Native men are more likely to die from cirrhosis than women, Native women have a higher death rate from cirrhosis than women in all other groups within the United States.[90] From 1992 to 1994, the sixth-leading cause of death for Native women was cirrhosis and chronic liver disease.[91]

Native women who were treated for alcohol-related issues identified depression, self-esteem, anger, and unresolved grief as negative side effects to drinking in studies conducted through the 1990s.[92] Unlike the recreational drinker and many adolescents, it may be important to consider addressing these issues identified by women in treatment programs specifically for Native women. Throughout Indian Country, Native providers, and in particular those working with battered women, have been increasingly disturbed by the lack of investigation and the decline in prosecutions in cases where sexual assault victims have been using alcohol. How investigators perceive Native women and adolescents as "legitimate victims" or less of a victim given alcohol use has not been studied and appears to be an area where more research and resources are needed. The manner with which Native women are viewed in their own communities is also an important factor to consider in understanding violence against Native women.

The Impact of the Tribal Community

The tribal community has a significant impact on how Native women are empowered, protected, or oppressed in their respective homelands. In both urban and tribal communities, isolation (physical, political, spiritual, and communal isolation) can entrap many Native women in violent relationships. In the early 1990s, Jeffrey D. Edelson and Michael D. Frank claimed that requesting assistance from an outsider or authority figure may be unacceptable for many rural women because of cultural norms of self-sufficiency and taking care of problems within the family or community.[93] This may also be true for Native women in urban and rural areas—a circumstance often exacerbated by the lack of culturally competent law enforcement and victim assistance personnel. In many urban settings, language and culture may present challenges for Native women to access services and intervention. A more critical consideration for both urban and rural/reservation Native women may be avoidance of law enforcement and social services/mental health personnel in situations of violence against women. Many times abused women are concerned that state child protection services may become involved, resulting in the loss of their children. In reservation communities, tribal law enforcement officials can be viewed as either an appropriate or inappropriate avenue for intervention, depending on who the identified offender is and their relationship to the investigating law enforcement officer, family relationships, and/or current tribal leadership.

White Buffalo Calf Woman Society

Although the problems faced by Native women and children are vast, they are not insurmountable. Native women and tribal nations have risen to the call and are providing hope. Additionally, numerous grassroots organizations are working on these issues. One of the first Native American grassroots organizations to address domestic violence is the White Buffalo Calf Woman Society. The society was organized in 1979 by Tillie Black Bear and provided the first domestic shelter for battered women in South Dakota on the Rosebud Reservation. The shelter today serves approximately 200 women and 1,500 children per year. In 1998, Black Bear was honored for her more than twenty years of work in counseling victims, conducting workshops for batterers, and working with law enforcement. South Dakota's attorney general described her as "epitomizing the dedication required to help crime victims . . . young and old . . . who live in every corner of the state."[94]

Cangleska

Another innovative tribal domestic violence program is Cangleska, Inc. *Cangleska* means "medicine wheel" in Lakota. Located in Kyle, South Dakota, on the Pine Ridge Reservation, Cangleska was created in 1987 and is a culturally based social service that has proven to be very successful in reducing domestic violence. Much of its success is due to the women and men who work in this program. Karen Artichoker is the director and her staff, which includes Cecilia Firethunder, has been successful in their ability to include the support and participation of respected tribal men, support of the tribal council and courts, collaboration on tribal police training, and the development of all-encompassing intervention/prevention programs and publications. One of the most useful resource developments of Cangleska is the Sample Tribal Domestic Violence Code. The code is constructed to provide victims of domestic violence with safety and protection, to utilize the criminal justice system in setting standards of behavior within the family that is consistent with traditional Native values, and to prevent future violence through prevention and public education programs. There are a number of shelters in tribal communities and a significant percentage of those shelters are located in South Dakota. Yet the vast majority of tribes in Indian Country do not have shelters for women and their children. There are only twenty-five tribal shelters in the United States today.

Alaska, which is home to more than 230 Native communities, houses another model program designed to provide safety for women. Lynn Hootch directs the Emmonak Women's Shelter, located in Emmonak, Alaska. This shelter was formed in 1988 and has played a prominent role in addressing violence and sexual assault. Housed in a community rich in culture and

Sovereign Women
Strengthen
Sovereign Nations

"A nation is not defeated until the hearts of its women are on the ground. Then it is done, no matter how brave its warriors or how strong its weapons."

—Cheyenne proverb

A PROJECT OF CANGLESKA, INC.

722 ST. JOSEPH ST.
RAPID CITY, SD 57701
605-341-2050
FAX: 605-341-2472
1-877-RED-ROAD
(733-7623)

WOMEN ARE SACRED - THERE'S NO EXCUSE FOR DOMESTIC VIOLENCE
VIOLENCE AGAINST WOMEN IS NOT TRADITIONAL

Cangleska, Inc., located on the Pine Ridge Reservation in South Dakota, runs a battered women's shelter and provides help to victims of domestic violence. This poster exemplifies the reclaiming of the sacred in Native women and the idea that if tribes are to remain sovereign, then Native women must be protected in their own personal sense of sovereignty as well.

tradition, Lynn Hootch, Martha Gregory, Marlene Waska, JoAnn Horn, Priscilla Kameroff, and Elizabeth Redfox have worked to get their community involved in healthy and violence-free activities and programming. In 2003, the Emmonak

Women's Shelter was selected as one of five model programs identified by the Department of Justice Office for Victims of Crime.

Child Abuse

Another serious community challenge that needs to be addressed is the high rate of child abuse, specifically child sexual abuse among tribal communities. Traditionally children have always been highly valued within Native communities, and protections were in place to keep both children and women safe. With the introduction of forced federal boarding school policies in the 1880s, children were separated from their parents, families, and communities. In the words of Richard Pratt, the founder of Carlisle Indian School, the U.S. government was attempting to "Kill the Indian and save the man" by providing an education steeped in Euro-American ideology and tradition. When many young adults attempted to return home, they often found that they no longer fit within the Native community as a result of extensive assimilation and acculturation forced upon them within the boarding school settings.

Native adults and elders today continue to share their stories of institutionalized verbal and emotional abuse, physical abuse, sexual abuse, and torture. Perhaps most damaging was the interruption of traditional parenting practices and customs that served to promote balance and health and maintain a measure of safety for children. The impact of almost one hundred years of boarding school policy aimed at cultural genocide continues to resonate in symptoms of historical trauma still impacting Native communities today.[95]

Native children are overrepresented in founded cases of child abuse, placement in the child welfare system, and in child fatalities.[96] There was some indication in the late 1990s that Native children were underrepresented in child sexual abuse cases, while sources indicated that there was an increase in child sexual abuse. Identifying reliable and consistent data regarding child abuse of Native children is problematic for a number of reasons. There are multiple agencies that collect data: federal, state, and tribal. As Kathleen Earle and Amanda Cross discuss in their report on *Child Abuse and Neglect among American Indian/Alaska Native Children*, there are discrepancies in rates of child abuse from different sources within the same states for the same time period, some data sets counted one child more than once and inaccuracies in the census data for Native Americans was also noted. They also point out some data sets do not control for Hispanic ethnicity when making comparisons between white and Native children and this variable appears to have an impact on child-abuse rates in Native populations.[97] The complexities of how data is gathered when Native children are involved are a significant and concerning challenge. Regardless of the rates of child abuse, many victims of child abuse in tribal communities are limited in obtaining services or resources.

Native children today live in a variety of tribal communities: on Indian reservations and communities located on mesas, at the bottom of remote canyons, on the plains, rancherias, adjacent to urban areas, in woodland areas, urban communities, suburban communities, and tundra villages. In Alaska, many of these locations are accessible only by plane, which can limit, if not completely prohibit, services provided to Alaska Native child victims. Many Native children live in geographically isolated or rural communities. The complexities of jurisdiction in tribal communities with underfunded initiatives to investigate, intervene, and provide services to child victims in Indian Country is overwhelming. Placement, medical, and mental health treatment services are often hundreds of miles away for Native children. It is this isolation for some Native children that contributes significantly to the difficulties in providing mental health, medical services, follow-up, and even case investigation for child victims of sexual abuse in tribal communities.

For other tribal communities conducting investigations, holding offenders accountable, and adequate treatment for children and their families remain major challenges. Urban Native children face other challenges, including access to culturally competent services and providers. Native children, whether in urban, rural, suburban, or reservation communities, are not ordinarily interviewed in their Native language and most investigators and forensic interviewers are not literate in the local Native language.[98] When allegations of child abuse arise, the investigation may present potential speech and language issues from the onset. Some Native children may be able to best communicate in an investigation in their Native language irregardless of English literacy. How Native children chose to tell about their lives is critical, choice of language and narrative ability in response to forensic questioning styles may be significant and much more salient within investigations.[99] Adequate, appropriate, and culturally competent medical and mental health care and healing interventions, as well as effective prosecution in the investigation of child sexual abuse allegations is critical for Native children who continue to be the most underserved victims.

Rates of Abuse

Reports on the condition of Native children indicate that they encounter serious challenges. Native children are twice as likely to live in a rental and when they live in homes owned by their families those homes are worth less in value than homes owned by other groups. One in four Native children live in poverty and three in ten Native children live in single-parent households. The school drop-out rate is higher for Native Americans than for any other demographic group in the United States, and Native children have a higher need for special education than other children.[100] Native children also represent 2 percent of the children in foster and group home care and 3 percent of the child abuse and neglect fatalities, even though the Native population is only

1 percent of the United States' population.[101] Native Americans
and Asians were the only racial groups to experience increases,
while other groups experienced decreases in the rate of child
abuse and neglect of children under the age of 15 as recorded by
child protective services agencies in recent years. In 1999,
according to a Bureau of Justice Statistics Report on American
Indians and Crime, the increase in reported incidences for
Native Americans was more than three times the number for
Asian children, while the per-capita rate for Native Americans
was seven times that of Asian children. This report suggests that
the incidence of child abuse has decreased for some children,
while increases were reported for Native and Asian children.[102]

In 1995, Native Americans accounted for just fewer than 2
percent of the victims of child abuse and neglect from nationwide reports. And as noted above there is some indication that
these numbers are increasing. One in 30 investigated cases of
child abuse is substantiated, which means that abuse was identified. In order to understand the significance of these statistics, it
is helpful to compare the statistics to other ethnic groups: one
case in 30 is substantiated for African American children, 1 case
in 66 is substantiated for white children, 1 case in 80 for Hispanic
children, and 1 case in 209 is substantiated for Asian American
children.[103]

Trauma has been found to be an integral part of the lives
of many Native children. In a number of smaller surveys conducted in the 1990s, as many as 60 percent of Native teens
reported that they have experienced or witnessed a traumatic
event. Ten percent of Native teens reported sexual abuse and
by age 18 that percentage increased to 21.6 percent. It is often
the system response as well as the community's reaction that
has lasting impact for children and their families in Native
communities.

Child sexual abuse is a complex area of child maltreatment.
The dynamics of child sexual abuse, investigation procedures,
jurisdictional challenges, the trend for multidisciplinary

responses, and child development challenges all contribute to the complexity involved in child sexual abuse cases.[104] Providing an effective criminal justice response is an important aspect of intervention in protecting children and sending a clear message within any community. Prosecution of child sexual abuse in tribal communities has been a challenge for a number of different reasons: underfunding of law enforcement and the criminal justice system response, children may recant or are unable or unwilling to testify, families may oppose prosecution, lack of support from the community, limited evidence, and lack of suspect confessions. Kathleen Colburn Faller suggests when caretakers support children in child sexual abuse cases, the incidence of recanting the abuse incident may decrease.[105] Community collaboration and agency relationships demonstrate that issues involving child witnesses and the dynamics of child abuse and child sexual abuse in particular can be addressed much more effectively if the system response is functioning adequately.[106] Professionals on the front lines have no ability to change many of the factors that influence prosecution. However, multidisciplinary team functioning and advocating for adequate funding in the areas of treatment and criminal justice response are areas where tribes, professionals, federal agencies, and policy makers can have an impact. Some of the greatest challenges are the sustainability of child abuse initiatives, underfunded tribal initiatives to address child abuse, multijurisdictions, prosecution of offenders, community support, treatment for victims and offenders, burnout, and staff turnover.

Advocacy Centers and Shelters

In order to address both system issues and the specific needs of child victims in complex child abuse cases, Children's Advocacy Centers were started in the 1980s. Although little research has been conducted in this area, Children's Advocacy Centers are considered to be the best approach to the investigation and intervention in severe physical and child sexual abuse cases. There are well more than six hundred Children Advocacy Center initiatives in the United States at varying levels of development. And there are only a handful of fully functioning Children's Advocacy Centers in tribal communities that are providing a coordinated multidisciplinary response and trying to address the needs of child victims and their families in cases of severe abuse and child sexual abuse. Two of these Children's Advocacy Centers located in Indian Country were identified in 2003 as model programs by the Department of Justice Office for Victims of Crime.

Wiconi Wawokiya, is a co-located domestic violence shelter and Children's Advocacy Center. The women's shelter has been in place for more than ten years and the Children's Safe Place was started in 1998 as a Children's Advocacy Center program within Wiconi Wawokiya, located in Fort Thompson, South Dakota, and home to the Crow Creek Sioux Tribe.

The Children's Safe Place implemented a tribal telemedicine program called Second Opinion. This program allows a physician's assistant to provide a specialized child sexual abuse medical exam in remote tribal communities. The photographic documentation of the exam is transmitted over a computer to a physician in Sioux Falls, South Dakota, who specializes in child sexual abuse. The physician in Sioux Falls provides a second opinion on the physician assistant's medical findings. Telemedicine programs can provide critical technological capabilities to Native communities often isolated from specialized services. Services provided by the Children's Safe Place include forensic interviews, medical exams, assessment of findings, mental health referrals, shelter, spiritual healing, case tracking, long-term support, information, and education.

The Heart to Heart Children's Advocacy Center is located in Cherokee, North Carolina, home of the Eastern Band of Cherokee Indians, and it is the longest running Children's Advocacy Center in Indian Country. The program is prosecution-based and also provides culturally specific treatment services. The center conducts forensic interviews, provides mental heath services, victim advocacy, and refers children for medical exams as needed. The director of this center is also a law enforcement investigator who conducts the forensic interview of alleged child victims' onsite. Both of these Children's Advocacy Centers have long-standing directors who were the founders of their programs and thus have created program sustainability in ways that have clearly promoted their longevity, as well as their success in their respective tribal communities.

The Native American Children's Alliance, National Indian Child Welfare Association, and the Tribal Law and Policy Institute are all national Native organizations providing resources, outreach, policy development and training, and technical assistance to tribes regarding child maltreatment and tribal sovereignty.

Founded in 1999, the Native American Children's Alliance (NACA) is a national organization dedicated to promoting the development of Children's Advocacy Centers and multidisciplinary teams in tribal communities through program sustainability initiatives.[107] Burnout and staff turnover are two of the most common challenges sited for program closure and challenges in many tribal communities. In response to these issues, NACA provides a cross-mentoring model of tribal approaches to promote tribal program sustainability. Tribal program representatives come together several times a year to share, train, troubleshoot, support, and mentor workers from other child abuse programs from across Indian Country and Alaska Native communities. Program participants often comment that this is one of the most valuable meetings they attend all year. NACA's board consists exclusively of representatives from tribal programs and therefore is able to support, promote, and advocate more effectively for tribes sustaining child abuse initiatives in tribal communities.

The National Indian Child Welfare Association (NICWA) is a private, nonprofit organization that has successfully evolved from a regional program to a national program that provides information exchange, national training, community development, and public policy analysis regarding child abuse and neglect. NICWA is a member organization made up primarily of tribal governments, urban Indian social service programs, individuals who are both Native American and non-Native American, private organizations, and front-line NICWA staff.

The Tribal Law and Policy Institute is a nonprofit corporation located in Santa Monica, California, that provides education, research, training, and technical assistance programs which promote justice in Indian Country and the health, well-being, and culture of Native peoples. Among a number of initiatives, the Tribal Law and Policy Institute provides training and technical assistance to tribal programs involved in developing a more comprehensive tribal response to child abuse.

Despite the high numbers of cases and underfunded tribal initiatives involving violence against Native women and children, tribal community programs and national Native initiatives remain resilient and continue to provide hope for Native children, women, and tribal communities.

5

Native American Sacred and Ceremony

*Brother we do not wish to destroy your religion or
take it from you; we only want to enjoy our own.*
—*Red Jacket (Seneca)*[108]

THE MEANING OF RELIGION

The study of religion is one of the oldest sociological concerns, which has its roots in the nineteenth century. At that time, founders of the discipline saw religion as the mainspring of human societies, and they believed it explained major differences within and between societies. Religion explains existence—how the world came to be, how humans related to the world and forces around them, why humans die, and it validates and gives meaning to human action. Also, it helps reinforce human ability to cope with the fragility of human life, it provides security in an unpredictable world, and it heightens the intensity of shared experience and of social communion. Scholars found that in traditional societies, religion had been the fundamental basis for social unity and this is exceptionally true for Native ways of worship.

To understand tribal life, cultural continuance, and cultural maintenance in the twenty-first century it is critical to understand their relationship to the sacred and ceremony. Native sacred and ceremony is a more appropriate term to describe Native religion, because many tribes did not have a word for religion. In part, they do not use religion because they do not separate the sacred from the secular. In this chapter, the term *religion* is used because it is a commonly used word for spirituality, sacredness, and ceremony that describes Native spiritual life.

To understand contemporary social problems related to Native sacred traditions it is important to understand what Native religious traditions are. First is the knowledge there is not "one Native tradition" to represent Native religion. In essence, there are as many Native religions as there are separate Native tribal societies. Also, the term *Native American religion* has historically posed complex problems of description and interpretation due to a lack of knowledge. This lack of knowledge of Native spiritual life has resulted in the misunderstanding, prohibition, and misappropriation of Native spirituality.

Native Religious Rituals and Ceremonies

Native rituals and ceremonies are so different that at times it is impossible to discuss them as one. They do, however, share two common elements: 1) Native religions are inseparable from Native culture, and 2) Native faith entails many complex interrelationships with both the forms and forces of their environment. Apart from these shared themes, Native ways of worship incorporate a wondrous variety of beliefs, sacraments, and systems. Some of these tribal beliefs parallel those of Western religions. For example, most tribes have distinct views of the supernatural world, with various deities and spirits, and many Native groups share a belief in one Supreme Being known by many names, such as Wakan Tanka (Sioux), Great Manitou (Chickasaw), Yusen (Apache), and Creator. Included in their similarities is the fact that their religious ways change. This is a very important topic because no religion stands still while the world changes around it. Native religions were thus quite charismatic and innovative, modifying and even replacing older traditions with new revelations.

Revitalization Movements

European and American colonization of indigenous peoples is fraught with conflict, which continues to be felt today. Early explorers, colonizers, and settlers depicted, through art and writings, Native Americans as heathens: they lacked civilized knowledge or will, lived a life of bestial self-fulfillment directed by instinct, and were ignorant of God and morality. The idea that Native people were without a religion dominated European thinking about Native Americans and was well-developed in the literature on the Spanish, French, and English conquest and settlement of the Americas.

One reaction to the attacks upon Native spirituality was the rise of revitalization movements. Native revitalization movements were innovative, and extreme efforts were developed to seek spiritual and material relief from chaos, hopelessness, and social destruction. This cultural stress resulted from the loss of lands, the depletion of game, broken treaties, and the eventual confinement to reservations. Native American revitalization movements emphasized the elimination of alien customs and values, stressed the restoration of traditional customs and values, transformation of society, and for some an expectation of an apocalyptic transformation of society and culture engendered by supernatural powers. Native revitalization began in the 1600s and continued into the 1800s. During the early movements, Native Americans

sought to reestablish their cultures and to restore their previ-
ous population levels. For various reasons, the early Native
revitalization movements did not succeed in removing the
oppressors from Native lands or in returning to the "old
ways."

Native revitalization in the late nineteenth century changed its characteristics. These new Native movements turned to
beliefs in supernatural powers to replace political and military
means to secure the renewal of Native culture. Late-nine-
teenth-century religious revitalization movements were larger
and lasted longer than the earlier ones. Both in geographic
extent and the number of Native Americans involved, the later
undertakings were more substantial than earlier ones and
expanded beyond tribal needs to seek a broader unity based on
shared needs and experiences. In the post-Civil War decades,
six revitalization movements occurred among Western
American Indians: the Prophet Dance, Smohalla's Dreamer
Religion of the Columbia River Plateau, the Indian Shakers of
Puget Sound, the Ghost Dance of 1870, the Ghost Dance of
1890, and the Peyote Cult. Two of the prophets of these religions—Smohalla and Wovoka—are still revered. Three of the
religions—the Dreamer Religion, the Shakers, and the Peyote
Religion—exist to this day, largely undisturbed in matters of
doctrine and ritual.

Another strategy for keeping their culture alive and to
maintain a culture in an ever-changing world was the move
toward syncretic ways. Upon contact with other Native tribes
and Euro-Americans, many Native Americans fought with varied success to retain their ancestral ways. The retention of their
traditional religions depended on their history and the extent
of their contact with other tribal religions and later with
Western religions. The reaction to their evolving societies took
several forms, including the practice of Native religious ways in
conjunction with elements of Christianity. Syncretism, the
combination of different forms of belief or practices, occurred

among Native traditions throughout the United States and among Eastern and Western religions.

During European contact, the world of Native Americans changed dramatically and their lives became more oppressed. Hence, their search and need for freedom and social cohesion became essential. The joining of other religious traditions with Native rites enabled many Native people to improve their lives by using the good in the various religious traditions. The syncretic ways of worship among Native peoples is vast and can be found among the Plains Sioux and throughout the Puget Sound region, where the Indian Shaker Religion was founded by John Slocum, a member of the Squaxin band. The Indian Shaker Religion applied Catholic, Protestant, and Native practices in its ceremonies. Similar to Catholics, Indian Shakers would make the sign of the cross numerous times a day, use candles, and hang up pictures of Roman Catholic saints in their homes. Protestant elements included in the Indian Shaker Religion were hymnals and a strong form of the Protestant work ethic. Indian Shakers were instructed to work hard and to stop drinking, gambling, betting, horse racing, and using tobacco. Native traditions manifested themselves in the Indian Shaker Religion through their curing of the sick. Although the religion had replaced the "medicine man," the ritual performance was very similar to the methods employed by Native healers. When someone was ill, members of the church rang bells over the place where the sickness was supposed to be, while other members would kneel on the floor and hold up their hands with candles in them. The Shakers believed that they were helping the bell-ringer extract the sickness. Local residents noted how Native participation in the Indian Shaker Church helped keep the people together and helped rebuild a sense of community.

Religious Equality

In efforts to keep Native traditions alive and people united in the twenty-first century, Native Americans have pushed the courts and Congress to help seek religious equality, particularly as it relates to traditional practices. After years of documentation of the prohibition, intrusion, and misunderstanding of Native religious ways, congressional action was taken on August 12, 1978. Noting how Native traditional religions are the fabric of Native American cultures, President Jimmy Carter signed the American Indian Religious Freedom Act (1978), Senate Joint Resolution 102, marking one of the most significant events in the long struggle of American Indian religious liberty. Carter strongly believed that it is a fundamental right of every American to worship as she or he pleases. The American Indian Religious Freedom Act (AIRFA) is one of the few instances in America's history when Congress granted to Indians their full legislative religious liberty. The purpose of AIRFA is to insure that policies and procedures affecting the exercise of traditional Indian religions be brought into compliance with First Amendment rights. This act created hope among Native people that a more tolerant and sensitive time had begun, but years later it proved to be ineffective because there was no accountability and no civil penalty was imposed if First Amendment rights were denied.

The right to worship as one pleases is a critical component of social unity but another important social issue faced by tribal communities is the desecration of sacred lands and objects. Native people have confronted this with vigor and through the courts. It is important to first realize that every religion has a place that it holds to be sacred. Believers throughout the world honor physical locations where they sense a divine presence. But for Native people, problems have come about because it is often difficult to determine the precise location of an Indian sacred site. Each tribe retains its unique sites, which may include a location mentioned in oral stories; a place where something supernatural has happened; a site where plants, land, and waters may possess healing powers; and/or a place where one communicates with the supernatural world. The issue of land has therefore become an area of conflict between Native and non-Native people, particularly when related to the treatment and use of sacred Indian lands.

Sacred Places

An example of the importance of sacred lands to Native Americans can be seen in the ninety-seven-year struggle waged by the Taos Pueblos over Blue Lake in northern New Mexico. The Pueblos argued that 1) religion was central to their life; 2) the Blue Lake area was essential to their religion; and 3) continued denial of access to the area threatened the existence of their culture. Symbolically, Blue Lake was considered the source of all Taos life and the retreat for souls after death. Annual pilgrimages are made to Blue Lake as part of an ancient ritual. The pilgrimage is a trek of fifteen to twenty miles to the lake shrine, where prayers are offered for the universal welfare of all people and for guidance and harmony in the spirit world. Blue Lake holds the same significance for the Taos people as a church holds for its parishioners. The mountain provides a sanctuary for religious activities, and is also a place for recreation, hunting, and herb gathering. Blue Lake was taken from the Pueblos in 1906 and became part of Carson National Forest. On December 15, 1970, President Nixon signed a bill returning Blue Lake and its surrounding lands to the Taos Pueblos. He spoke of how the Pueblos had legal rights to the land and attested that his action "involved respect for religion."

Sacred Objects

Another social issue that Native Americans encounter today is the destruction, theft, and disrespect of Native spiritual objects. Native Americans have a number of sacred objects that are imbued with special significance and are used by traditional Native religious leaders during the practice of traditional Native American religions. The use, possession, and access to

For nearly a century, the Taos Pueblos struggled to regain control of New Mexico's Blue Lake, where they believe their people originated and go to when they die. Though a number of bills passed in the U.S. House of Representatives, they never made it past the Senate, thanks to opposition by New Mexico Senator Clinton P. Anderson. Finally, in 1970 Congress passed the Harris-Griffin Bill, which was signed into law by President Nixon (shown here). The bill returned 48,000 acres of land to the Taos Pueblos.

vital sacred objects have proven difficult in some areas, especially the sacramental use of peyote. Peyote is a small, low-growing hairy cactus, whose flesh is eaten. The flesh looks like a small pincushion when dried like a button. It grows in Texas and Mexico. Native definitions of peyote vary with some believing that it is power, a bible, and medicine for the mind, body, and soul. Early Americans, though, defined it as an illegal drug. The peyote ceremony also varies but generally it is an all-night ceremony held in tepees, hogans, houses, and/or apartments, consisting of four major elements: prayer, singing, eating the peyote, and quiet contemplation. Some ceremonies incorporate elements of Christianity, but the inclusions varied from tribe to tribe. Native Americans participate in this ceremony for a number of reasons, such as curing, good learning, guidance, securing good fortune for children, and safety of soldiers. Many Native Americans also turned to peyote as a way to stop drinking alcohol.

Among those who fought for the use of the sacred sacrament was Quanah Parker (1852–1911), a Comanche chief who testified before the Oklahoma State Legislature in 1908 and in later years in front of federal courts. The court case *People v. Woody* (1964) was a strong and positive signal in the struggle for legal protection of Native ceremonies and traditional rites. In rendering its decision, the Supreme Court concluded:

1) That since the use of peyote incorporates the essence of religious experience and that peyote presents only a slight danger to the state and enforcement of its laws, the scales of justice are unquestionably in favor of First Amendment rights.

2) The right of free religious expression embodies a precious heritage of our history and it should be recognized and respected for all cultures.

3) They believed that its decision preserved more than an ancient tradition but the rights of Indians who honestly practiced an old religion.

The courts in *Oregon v. Smith* (1990) broke away from the well-established precedent set in *Woody,* in which the interests of state and Indian religious rights were weighed (Balancing Test). Writing for the court, Supreme Court Justice Antonin Scalia wrote that America's religious diversity is a "luxury" that a pluralistic society cannot afford, and he recommended that religious practitioners look elsewhere to Congress or state legislatures for protection of their practices, instead of the courts and the Bill of Rights. This ruling dramatically departed from well-established First Amendment rights and is incompatible with our nation's commitment to individual religious liberty. In an effort to define peyote use rights, on October 6, 1994, President Clinton signed the American Indian Religious Freedom Act Amendment of 1994 (Public Law 103-344). The amendment holds that the use, possession, or transportation by an Indian of peyote for bona fide ceremonial purposes in connection with the practice of a Native American religion by an Indian is lawful and shall not be prohibited by the federal government or any state. No Indian shall be penalized or discriminated against on the basis of such use, possession, or transportation, including but not limited to denial of otherwise applicable benefits under public assistance programs.

Native Cultural Appropriation

One of the most pressing issues confronting Native Americans in the twenty-first century, which is considered to be detrimental to Native life and culture, is the appropriation of Native spirituality. This is a complex issue whereby both Native and non-Native people are to blame. Native cultural appropriation is defined as taking Native spirituality and claiming it as one's own. It occurs when someone else speaks for, tells, defines, describes, represents, uses, or recruits the images, stories, experiences, or dreams of Native Americans for their own. Native cultural appropriation is becoming an especially large problem in urban areas.

Detrimental impacts can be felt within tribes and between Native Americans and non-Natives. Onondaga spiritual leader Oren Lyons has called for the stop of cultural appropriation and for the need for more intercultural respect today. Many Native Americans find it inappropriate for non-Native Americans to carry sacred objects because the objects were given to "the people" and the purpose and procedures are specific to their time. Intercultural issues exist regarding Native and non-Native Americans posing as spiritual leaders without the consent of the tribe. It has been noted that "real" medicine people are chosen by the medicine and long instruction, and tribal-specific discipline is necessary before ceremonies and healing can be done. These procedures are always carried out in the Native tongue; there are no exceptions and profit is not the motivation. While some Native Americans seek to educate the rest of America about their culture, others are drawing a line. To them, learning about a culture doesn't give non-Native Americans the right to appropriate symbols and ritual for their own profit. Harmful outcomes include the rejection and disrespect of "real" spiritual leaders and the exploitation and commercialization of Native cultures. Others have viewed the mainstreaming of Native spirituality as a cancer and say it hinders true Native spiritual leaders as they struggle to revitalize Native practices among their own people. When people play at being Indians, it takes attention away from the real needs of Native people. Also, the possession, use, and creation of "pipes" as an income-producing form of arts and crafts is sacrilegious. This area is also a concern to many as Native Americans continue to see the commodification of sacred items, such as kachinas, pipe stone, and many tribal specific symbols.

Many Native Americans are deeply spiritual and the appropriation of their religious ways, which is a means to unity, strength, healing, and continuance, is considered an assault on their culture, leading them to think that there is absolutely nothing—pipes, dances, land, water, feathers, drums, and even prayers—that non-Native Americans cannot take whenever and wherever they wish. Visions, prayers, etc., that used to be private tribal practices are now becoming public. Several tribes have passed codes addressing this issue, many of which can be found on the internet.

Urban Native Americans have been appropriators, as well as participants, as they attempt to fill a religious void that they have encountered living away from their ancestral lands. Being

Appropriation of Native American cultural items is becoming a growing problem, especially in urban areas of the United States. Sacred objects, such as kachinas and pipe stone, are used in religious ceremonies and many Native Americans feel it is inappropriate for the general public to possess these items. Shown here is a Navajo kachina made of silver.

removed from traditional life created much stress for urban Native Americans, and as a way to recreate community they began to participate in powwows (a social activity that has its roots in traditional ceremonies) in cities. Powwows, today, have become commercialized and vibrant. They can last for several days and are often held at Indian Centers, universities, schools, and parks, and are largely considered pan-Indian events. This type of event helps maintain Native identity, values, reinforces the importance of Native socializing, and erases feelings of loneliness. However, powwows have traditionally created factionalism. They have been viewed negatively as a pan-Indian movement that is the work of mixed-bloods and assimilated Native Americans who have lost their "true" tribal identities. But most Natives see powwows as fostering cultural revitalization, promoting national identity, and helping preserve traditional ways. Spiritual components that remain an integral part of Native sacred and ceremony are Native prayer and dancing. At powwows, prayer is used at the beginning of all opening grand entries and dancing, which includes both traditional and non-traditional. Native dancing had once been outlawed and viewed as a "pagan" act but it continues into the twenty-first century.

Searching for an Identity

The question of what constitutes an "American Indian" is fraught with conflict and complexity, and has been a point of contention for many Native Americans. This struggle to find an identity has become even more difficult when the chosen identity is both Native and Christian. For too long Native Christian voices have been ignored by scholars because most academics remain focused on the study of Native tribal religions. A major reason for the lack of studies of Native Christian discourses is that "Indianness" is usually tied to simplicity and tradition, rather than the complexities of change and history. To many people, Christian Native Americans have been seen as unauthentic and assimilated. To others, however, Christian Native Americans are agents in their own religious destinies. The incorporation of Christianity into tribal life has also caused factionalism between traditionalists and Christian Native Americans, with the perception that Christianity is a threat to tribalism.

Defining what an "Indian" is has become a critically important and complex question that many Native Americans are attempting to address, because it is tied to well-being, resources, membership, and services. This need to define what "Indian" means has plagued many Native Americans, particularly Christian Indians.

By the mid-nineteenth century, many Native Americans had adopted Christianity. The reasons for conversion varied a great deal from place to place. It can easily be argued that conversion was coerced and at times forced. But this is a simplistic notion. Motives for spiritual changes are vast and complex. In some cases, the similarities between traditional Native religious ways and Christianity removed the pressure for conversion. For example, both Native worlds and Christianity depended upon mediation powers of guardian spirits or saints and both found the way to the sacred through ritual. In other instances, Indians followed white ways because of Indian prophecies that discussed the coming of white men who had access to supernatural powers, power that Native people sought to claim. The friendships between missionaries and Native Americans also promoted conversion. Some Native people searched and obtained help from missionaries who were against detrimental Indian policies, corrupt Indian agents, and exploitative frontiersmen.

Arguably, a change from traditional forms of worship is tied to the attitude that the exchange will lead to better social and cultural lifestyles. For some, Christianity provided immediate freedom from disorder and destruction, whereas for others it gave them a sense of security and safety through the acceptance and love of God. Another justification for its acceptance was that it promised to fill a spiritual vacuum, which resulted from cultural deterioration. By facilitating the acquisition of material goods, Christianity helped Native

Americans resolve the physical and psychological stress caused by European contact. Christianity brought many Native Americans opportunities for belief in a different kind of revivalism, one which expressed itself in terms of general salvation of Indians and other races. Likewise, it offered the prospect of a perfect world in which both living and dead would be reunited without the ills of worldly suffering.

Prior to contact, Native people had their own cultural and religious systems that sustained their well-being for centuries. However, with the arrival of European colonizers came the suppression and prohibition of traditional Native religious practices. In an attempt to "civilize" the Indians, the colonizers sought to undermine traditional ways of worship. To Europeans one could not be civilized unless one was Christianized. Euro-Americans strongly believed that "to educate the Indian in the ways of civilized life . . . was to preserve him from extinction, not as an Indian, but as a human being."[109] Facing such strong policies aimed at destroying traditional ways of worship, many Native Americans converted to Christianity and denied all that was Native. The voices of these colonized Native Americans are void of tribal time and tribal culture. These Christian Indians spoke of their ways as being pagan and would present the religions of their fathers as devil worship with no value. Other Christian Native Americans provide a "hybrid" perspective, which includes tribal and Christian orientation. Writings from these Native people became apparent around the 1930s. They struggled with the contradictions and difficulties of denying the faith of their fathers—a faith that had sustained their people for hundreds of years. They would praise both Native and Christian spiritual ways.

The relationship between Native people and Christianity has changed over the years with a move toward a more analytical assessment of Christianity and a quest for mutual understanding. The impetus for further questioning has come from the historical and continual assault by Christians who saw Native Americans as godless people who had to be saved from themselves. For centuries, Christian Native Americans have struggled with the acceptance of their culture, heritage, and Indianness in conjunction with God in their lives. Today, there is a new movement—as Native Christians move into the twenty-first century, they are people well enmeshed in American society and are well equipped to confront and discuss the conflicts that arise from being Native and Christian, and the need for a more inclusive Christian theology.

One of the most sophisticated Native writers in the twentieth century, Vine Deloria, Jr., has addressed these issues in many of his writings. Deloria is the son of an Episcopal priest and a graduate of the Lutheran School of Theology and the University of Colorado School of Law. His outstanding works serve as cornerstones in the debates concerning Christian doctrines and Native beliefs. Thanks in part to Deloria's books, *Custer Died for Your Sins* (1969) and *God is Red* (1973), Native people began to seek a more meaningful Christian theology. Deloria insisted at that time that the teachings of Christian churches were obsolete in the twentieth century because they did "not provide the understanding with which society makes sense. Nor did Christian teachings provide any means by which the life of the individual has value." In his early writings, Deloria urged national denominations to "assist in the creation of a national Indian Christian Church" that included "all ordained Indian clergymen." As a strong believer in the values of Native spirituality, Deloria felt that "an Indian version of Christianity" and creation of new forms of a ministry would benefit Indian societies—ministries that are not "determined by obsolete theological distinctions preserved from the middle ages" but ministries that reflect the culture and needs of the people they serve.

Deloria's attitude toward Christianity has hardened over the years, and today he prefers and believes that tribal religions are superior to Christianity. But his early assertion that if Christianity is to be practiced, it should be more connected to the land and the people of that land—a belief that continues to speak to many Native Christians. Furthermore, Deloria claims that God supports both North American land and its indigenous people—proposing the belief that "God is Red." Deloria continues to support the move toward a new Native theology. Following Deloria's earlier writings, many contemporary Native Christians are claiming their conversions and making them their own. This action creates a Native view of Christ and his teachings and a break from the bondage of the gospel as interpreted by Eurocentric values and ideas. Native Christians have accomplished this through the development of resource materials that provide a Native or indigenous articulation of Christian theology, affirm the relevance of tribal cultures, and help bridge the gap between Native and non-Native cultures. As Native Americans move into the twenty-first century, they are reinterpreting Christian theology and biblical interpretation to include human differences, and through this act they are defining for themselves what it means to be Native and Christian. Through a new outlook, Christian Native Americans have transformed their patterns of worship to be culturally appropriate, which provides them the spiritual base necessary for health and well-being for themselves and their communities. There remains, however, residues of Eurocentric attitudes and values in many churches that subjugate Native Christians. But because they believe that they are free in Jesus Christ, many Christian Native Americans persist in their fight to be free from those old notions. Today, they assert their independence to abandon their Native traditions or freedom to incorporate them into their Christian teachings as a means of survival.

In sum, Native sacred traditions are as complex as the people and communities in which they come from—and many social concerns and issues derive from them. What is most important is the continued struggle for Native people to preserve traditional values and beliefs, not only against federal and state laws restricting them but also against cultural appropriators, because Native religions are the essence of tribal survival, identity, and continuance.

6

Cultural Resources

When we think of historical preservation, I suppose that you think of
something that is old, something that has happened in the past and
that you want to put away on a shelf
and bring it out and look at every now and then. . . .
In our way of thinking, everything is a significant event,
and the past is as real as us being here right now.
—Paris Butler, Fort Mohave[110]

PROTECTING NATIVE AMERICAN CULTURE

Indian nations have had a continuous and historical struggle in the protection of tribal religions and cultural resources. The continued success and protection of tribal resources may ultimately impact the cultural maintenance of social health and balance in tribal communities. This chapter discusses cultural resources and many of the federal laws that impact tribal cultural resources. Native religion, tribal sovereignty, and government-to-government relationships are also critical and foundational areas to cover in the discussion of tribal cultural resources. Tribal cultural resources will be considered in a number of different areas. First, there are sacred sites located on federal lands in which federal agencies are directed to accommodate access to and ceremonial use of these sites by Native religious practitioners and, where appropriate, maintain confidentiality of the sacred site. An area of extensive tribal involvement continues to be over the protection of human remains and items buried with them—cultural and sacred objects—whether they are found in museums, are at risk of being currently uncovered on federal lands, or have been dug up from burial grounds in the past. The Native American Graves Protection and Repatriation Act protects the cultural interests of tribes with respect to burials, and cultural and sacred objects, and requires a return of these to the rightful owners defined under this law. Another area that involves cultural resources is the area of traditional cultural places or properties. These include a district, site, building, structure, or object that a human community places value on.[111] Traditional cultural places or properties are "historically rooted and figure importantly in the lives of communities."[112] There are laws that protect places and properties when they have particular meaning for communities.

An aspect of tribal property that has significant value and is often difficult to protect is the area known as "intellectual property," which may include issues of trademark, copyright, or ownership rights regarding culture, language, names, songs, dances, sacred teachings, and other traditional knowledge. The unique aspect of many tribal property interests and cultural resources involves the idea that tribes claim to own property collectively. Tribes often claim that cultural resources do not belong to one individual but instead they belong to the community and it is the group that has control over the various types of property produced by their community. There are many problems that arise in this area, which include the fact that many people do not recognize cultural property, or in some way disrespect it.

Cultural resources is a broad and complex topic and this chapter will include a discussion of tribal sovereignty, government-to government relations, sacred sites, religious freedom, consultation, history of the federal cultural resource law, the Native American Graves Protection and Repatriation Act, and traditional cultural places or properties.

Traditionally, Native peoples within the United States practiced a land-based religion and utilized a vast number of cultural items. These traditional practices continue today irrespective of the introduction of Christianity and assimilation

Pu'u o Mahuka Heiau

The Pu'u o Mahuka *Heiau* (a religious site or temple) is the largest site of its kind on the Hawaiian island of O'ahu. Pu'u o Mahuka, which means "hill of escape," is located in the Waimea Valley, on the north shore of the island. The site was most likely established during the seventeenth century, and during the precontact period it was a major center on O'ahu, playing an important role in the political, social, and religious aspects of the area. The original structure was some twenty feet in height, and consisted of an alter (*tele*), an oracle tower (*anu'u*)—a kind of steeple—and images of the creator god (ki'i). The floor was lined with basalt and coral boulders, and smaller stones (*'ili'ili*) were later placed on top of these boulders. Religious services were held at the anu'u, and the gods were said to speak to the kahuna (priests) and the ali'i nui (high ruling chief).

Today, visitors to the four-acre site, which was made a National Historic Monument in 1962, are urged not to walk on the rock walls, and move or remove the stones from these structures. The importance of maintaining and providing Native Hawaiians access to *heiaus*, among other sacred sites, is critical in promoting and sustaining Native Hawaiian community and culture. Many Native Hawaiians still pray and leave offerings at sites like Pu'u o Mahuka Heiau.

into mainstream America. For many tribes, religion and cultural practices exist on federal, state, and public lands, because many sacred sites and traditional cultural properties are located there. Tribes that were removed or relocated from their homelands have encountered many problems, because traditional cultural properties, such as graves, sacred sites, and gathering places, are now located on federal, state, or public lands that may be located far from their present land base, thereby prohibiting their protection and use.

These lands are threatened by the multiple uses and users that may be involved in mineral mining, federal projects, recreation and tourism, or other competing federal and public land uses. Federal agencies and federal personnel are currently responsible for the administration of policy on public and federal lands and therefore must manage the competing users of these lands. Today, federal personnel must consider the implications for tribes with regards to government-to-government relations, natural and cultural resources, consultation, sacred sites, cultural use of the natural environment, traditional cultural properties, and the Native American Graves Protection and Repatriation Act of 1990.[113] When cultural resources exist on tribal lands, the conflicts are somewhat different than when the tribe's cultural resources are located on federal or public lands.

Cultural resources can be things that have cultural character like historic places, artifacts, documents, and social institutions. Oftentimes tribal communities are most concerned about Native graves and cultural items, sacred sites, religious practices, historic resources, protecting traditional and tribal knowledge, cultural use of natural resources, archaeological resources, and cultural use of the natural environment. Indian tribes, unlike other ethnic populations in the United States, have a special status as indigenous peoples and are able to assert their rights to protect their cultural resources by using a variety of specific laws and policies.

Government-to-Government Relationship

Federally recognized tribes in the United States manage and run their own governments, schools (or control local school boards), newspapers, radio stations, court systems, businesses, tourism departments, transportation programs, and a variety of community programs as a function of their sovereign status. Tribal sovereignty is extra-constitutional, meaning it existed before the creation of the U.S. Constitution and before the formation of the United States. The United States affirmed the sovereign status of tribes in a court case decided in 1831, *Cherokee Nation v. Georgia,* which emphasized that tribes like states are considered sovereign entities within the United States despite their status as "domestic dependent nations."[114] This sovereign status is critical to understanding how and why tribes are able to protect and manage their cultural resources.

The rights to manage their own affairs and deal with the United States was strengthened further on April 29, 1994, when President Clinton implemented the policy that was articulated in a presidential memorandum, "Government-to-Government Relations with Native American Tribal Governments."[115] The unique legal relationship with tribal governments was acknowledged in this formal document by the executive branch of the federal government. This policy was implemented to emphasize the importance the executive branch's role is in dealing with tribes on a government-to-government basis and the importance of recognizing and respecting the sovereign status of tribes. Because tribes have extensive interaction with federal agencies, President Clinton outlined principles that federal agencies would follow in their dealings with tribal governments as they sought to undertake activities that could impact or affect tribal governments. This policy of government-to-government relations is intended to make the interactions between federal agencies and tribal governments respectful and successful and it lays out the responsibilities for the protection and access to Native American cultural

In 1994, then-President William J. Clinton implemented a policy that recognized the U.S. government's unique legal relationship with tribal governments. Clinton's presidential memorandum served to make the relationship between the federal government and tribes more respectful and successful. Clinton is shown here at the White House with former Cherokee Nation chief Wilma Mankiller and Gaiashkibos, former chairman of the Lac Courte Oreilles Chippewa.

resources. Outlined in the policy were six basic principles that were intended to be used to guide federal agencies in their interactions with tribes:

1) The head of each executive department and agency shall be responsible for ensuring that the department or agency operates with a government-to-government relationship with federally recognized tribal governments;

2) Each executive department and agency shall consult, to the greatest extent practicable and to the extent permitted by law, with tribal governments

prior to taking actions that affect federally recognized tribal governments. All such consultations are to be open and candid so that all interested parties may evaluate for themselves the potential impact of relevant proposals;

3) Each executive department and agency shall assess the impact of federal government plans, projects, programs, and activities on tribal trust resources and assure that tribal government rights and concerns are considered during the development of such plans, projects, programs, and activities;

4) Each executive department and agency shall take appropriate steps to remove any procedural impediments to working directly and effectively with tribal governments on activities that affect the trust property and/or governmental rights of the tribes;

5) Each executive department and agency shall work cooperatively with other federal departments and agencies to enlist their interest and supporting cooperative efforts, where appropriate, to accomplish the goals of this memorandum; and

6) Each executive department and agency shall apply the requirements of Executive Orders Nos. 12875 ("Enhancing the Intergovernmental Partnership") and 12866 ("Regulatory Planning and Review") to design solutions and tailor federal programs, in appropriate circumstances, to address specific or unique needs of tribal communities.[116]

In essence, there needs to be respectful dialogue between federal agencies and tribes. The relationship will vary from tribe to tribe given the differences of cultures and traditions but it is important that the ongoing relationship begin with the tribes at the earliest stage. For example, the Department of the

Navy has worked with tribes regarding access to sacred herbs and medicines that are located on Naval installations, as well as access to Native sacred sites.

Protection of Sacred Sites

One of the areas of great concern for tribes and often an area of conflict with non-Native Americans involves the protection of sacred sites. On May 24, 1996, President Clinton signed Executive Order 13007, Indian Sacred Sites.[117] Executive orders function like laws or statutes, except that they originate from the executive branch, which is under the power of the president. Similar to many areas of the law, and the U.S. Constitution in particular, protections are embedded in the law to guarantee certain protections to our citizens. However, the protection of Native property and interests, whether in treaties, the U.S. Constitution, or other agreements, have been compromised by the federal government and federal policies throughout history. As a result, separate laws have been passed that specifically protect tribal interests even though a more general law may already exist that protects these same interests. For example, under the establishment clause of the First Amendment to the Constitution, our federal government is prohibited from interfering with Native religious practices in the United States.

AIRFA

In 1978, the American Indian Religious Freedom Act (AIRFA) was passed to recognize past violations and provide protection for Native religious practices.[118] However, that has not been the case historically. The federal government has violated this protection by forcibly prohibiting—through the use of the military—both the Sun Dance and Ghost Dance ceremonial practices occurring in tribal communities in the early twentieth century. Under AIRFA, the federal government is prohibited from establishing or prohibiting the free exercise of Native religion. Instead the government has a duty to recognize and consider religious practices and places in federal planning efforts. AIRFA itself does not direct federal agencies to do anything in particular but agencies need to consider what impact their actions will have on religious places under AIRFA and another law, the National Environmental Policy Act (NEPA), Section 106. Even though the U.S. Constitution guarantees citizens the right to practice religion without interference from the government, AIRFA was passed to address and uphold religious freedom for Native Americans.

NEPA

In the National Environmental Policy Act under Section 106, federal agencies must take into account the effects of their actions on historic properties; and afford the Advisory Council a reasonable opportunity to comment on their actions. Understanding and respecting the importance of sacred sites, traditional cultural properties, and plant-gathering for spiritual purposes require an appreciation of a different worldview or way of thinking about religion. Native practice of religion is very different than Christian worship, which occurs mostly within a church conveniently located to parishioners. Perhaps that is why it is so difficult for many Americans to truly understand and respect Native religious practices. Federal agencies must consider and consult with tribes regarding their actions and potential impacts on tribal interests. Federal agencies are not required under the law to go along with the tribes.

Blue Lake or "Ba Whyea," which was previously mentioned on page 73, is a sacred site for the Taos Pueblos, located in Taos, New Mexico. The federal government appropriated Blue Lake in 1906 even though the 1848 Treaty of Guadalupe Hidalgo—which ended the Mexican War—acknowledged that Taos land ownership included Blue Lake. The Pueblos protested for sixty-four years and in 1970, the lake was restored to them. The Taos origin story tells of how the tribe was created out of the waters of Blue Lake. The lake has been a part of the Taos Pueblos' daily life of worship. Today, only enrolled members of the Pueblo have access to the lake. Many non-Native Americans understand the enjoyment and recreation that occurs at a lake. However, seeing a lake as part of the religious origin of where people came from may be more of a challenge for non-Native Americans to understand and honor as a legitimate religious belief. Seferino Martinez, a former tribal leader, shares a Taos perspective on Blue Lake: "We don't have beautiful structures and we don't have gold temples in this lake, but we have a sign of a living god to whom we pray—the living trees, the ever-green and spruce, and the beautiful flowers and the beautiful rocks and the lake itself. We have this proof of sacred things we deeply love, deeply believe."[119] Seeing a lake as part of the religious origin of where a people came from may be more of a challenge for non-Native Americans to understand and truly honor as a legitimate religious belief.

Given how strongly tribes regard their own religion and traditional beliefs and the protection that the law affords tribes, it is critical for federal agency personnel to listen and consider a tribal perspective before taking action on projects that will impact tribal cultural resources. Consultation is discussed throughout this chapter, because there are laws, executive orders, and memoranda that direct federal agencies in a manner that requires consultation with tribes before taking action on projects where there may be an impact on tribal communities or tribal interests. An increasing number of federal statutes, executive orders, and memoranda require federal consultation with Indian tribes, Alaska Native Americans, and Native Hawaiian organizations. There is no definition of consultation within these laws and executive orders.

Archaeological Preservation by the U.S. Government
Historically, it can be argued that the federal government promoted desecration, rather than preservation. The oldest historic

and archaeological preservation statute is the Antiquities Act of 1906.[120] This act allowed the president to withdraw public lands to protect prehistoric and historic ruins, monuments, and other objects located on federal lands. The act was intended to preserve such sites, including Indian burial grounds, for later research by those holding federal permits. A permit to excavate could be obtained under the Antiquities Act by public museums, universities, or other specified educational institutions.

ARPA

In 1979, Congress passed the Archaeological Resources Protection Act (ARPA), which to many was also a discriminator like the Antiquities Act. ARPA has largely superseded the Antiquities Act and was enacted to "secure, for the present and future benefit of the American people, the protection of archaeological resources and sites which are on public lands and Indian lands." What should be noted is that ARPA defines Native American remains more than one hundred years old as "archeological resources" under this act. Defined as such, they may be dug up by a federal permit holder and the items that are recovered can be placed in storage in public museums and are then considered the property of the United States.

One positive aspect to ARPA is that it will not grant permits for the excavation or removal of archaeological resources on Indian lands until the permit holders receive the consent of the Indian owner or the tribe. ARPA also forbids the selling of any archaeological resource excavated or removed illegally from federal lands and provides penalties for noncompliance. It has a very progressive provision that "directs federal land managers to set up programs to increase public awareness of the significance of the archaeological resources and the need to protect such resources." While the Act protects sites from looting and prohibits excavations on federal lands without a federal permit, it does not apply to burial sites on state or private lands.

Select Committee on Indian Affairs

Legislation to establish a process for the repatriation of human and sacred objects had its origins in a hearing that was held by the Select Committee on Indian Affairs in February 1987. In this hearing, the secretary of the Smithsonian Institution indicated that of the 34,000 human remains in its collection, 42.8 percent or 14,523 of the specimens are the remains of North American Indians and another 11.9 percent or 4,061 of the specimens represent Inuit, Aleut, and Koniag populations. Tribal reaction to his statement was swift, and Indian tribes around the country called for the repatriation of those human remains with a specific tribe or region. When Congress decided to address the controversial issue of the possession and use of human remains held in the nation's museum, the National Congress of American Indians (the oldest and largest Indian organization in the United States) estimated that at least 600,000 Indian remains were residing in museums and universities. Other scholars estimated that museums, federal agencies, and private collectors had between 300,000 and 2.5 million Indian remains. Clearly, these are astounding numbers.

In response, Congress passed two federal repatriation laws. The first law, passed in 1989, affects the Smithsonian Institution, which is a national museum. It requires the museum to return human remains from its collection of 18,500 Native dead to appropriate tribes or groups as requested. This law signaled a turning point in the way that the federal government treats human remains of Native Americans. For the first time, the U.S. government recognized that Indian remains were human beings, not "archeological resources."

NAGPRA

The reburial movement finally won sweeping national reform on November 16, 1990, when President George H.W. Bush signed the Native American Graves Protection and

Repatriation Act (NAGPRA). NAGPRA was a new milestone in Indian and white relations.

NAGPRA covers five basic areas: 1) it protects Indian graves on federal and tribal lands; 2) it gives tribes control over the treatment of unmarked graves; 3) it prohibits the commercial selling of human remains; 4) it requires the inventory and repatriation of human remains held by the federal government and institutions that receive federal funding; and 5) it requires government and federally funded institutions to return stolen or improperly acquired sacred objects and other important communally owned property to Native owners.[121]

NAGPRA addressed essential human rights issues for Native Americans—a remarkable reflection of new attitudes in the American scientific community. But passage of the law was achieved only after many difficult battles over repatriation.

Archaeologists and physical anthropologists have emerged as the chief opponents to repatriation. They have been supported by the Society of American Archaeology and the American Anthropological Association, which argued that repatriation will "undermine scholarship." Archeologists study people and cultures of the past by examining artifacts, dwellings, and other physical or material evidence. Evidence found in burials contains a wide variety of information about the dead and the people who buried them.

Some archaeologists study the objects buried with the dead, such as pottery and jewelry, to learn about a culture. Other scientists are interested in the human remains found in graves. Skeletons are studied for information about gender, age, diet, nutrition, and disease. As Roger and Walter Echo-Hawk note in their book, *Battlefield and Burial Grounds: The Indian Struggle to Protect Ancestral Graves in the United States*: "The origin of archaeology in the United States is sometimes traced to Thomas Jefferson, who dug up an Indian burial mound in Virginia during the late 1700s. Despite American society's general respect for the death, Indian skeletons became objects of intellectual curiosity, valued as scientific research material."[122]

In response, many Native Americans and communities basically argued that any loss to science as a result of bone reburial was minor compared to human and religious rights. Most Native Americans believe that respect for the dead is more important than any knowledge of the past that might be gained by digging up graves. Tribes are also keenly aware that archaeological interest in human remains does not usually justify the digging up of graves of white Americans. This double standard about burials has long been a source of conflict between Native Americans and American archaeologists.

But many people have supported Native struggles for the return of their ancestors' bones and other items buried with them. Most museum directors concede that there will be some dissenters, but they believe that they will remain a minority. As it stands now, the passage of NAGPRA brought to an end one phase in the relationship between tribes and museums and began another, where relationships are undergoing additional changes.

NAGPRA deals with situations involving Native remains, objects, and cultural patrimony that may be housed in museum collections or discovered accidentally or purposefully during federal projects or activities. Under NAGPRA, consultation is required with Indian tribes, Native Hawaiian organizations, lineal descendants, and traditional Native American religious leaders in determining the disposition of human remains, funerary objects, sacred objects, and objects of cultural patrimony, when these remains and objects are in the control of or under the agency's possession. When objects or remains are repatriated (given back) it becomes the tribes, Native Hawaiian organizations, or lineal descendents' responsibility to decide what will ultimately happen with these possessions.

Tribal Historic Preservation Officers

Many tribes have Tribal Historic Preservation Officers (THPO) to increase and improve tribal access to input in the historic preservation system for their cultural resources. Tribes have a keen interest and take active roles in repatriation issues, protecting and gaining access to sacred sites, religious freedom, designations of traditional cultural properties, and gaining access for cultural use of natural resources. Vine Deloria reminds us that

> Native religious beliefs are not contained in just the land, mountains, and streams. The existence of the spirit world that connects the land to the other side is also what makes sense of place sacred. A lot of Native ceremonies involve going out onto the land to gain insight to revelations and wisdom that can come to people in prayer, vision quests, sweat lodges or other ceremonies. What is unique and powerful about Native religious practices for Indians and non-Indians alike is how this wisdom or insight tells people how to move, live and understand our world. It is difficult for many non-Indians to understand how a process such as this could be religion and not recreation.[123]

Native Americans aren't asking for exclusive rights to the land but often tribes are promoting how important it is for the land to be preserved for the sacred use of a particular area, mountain, stream, or landscape. The general public, judges deciding these cases, as well as others do not believe this is a real religion because of their own worldview that religion happens within the framework of a church, not the natural unaltered landscape of nature. Religion in this way in the mainstream is completely connected to the physical institution of a church.[124] It seems more difficult for the general public to respect and take seriously a Native sacred place that occurs in nature because the mainstream view on religion is tied so strongly to church-based worship. In many areas of the country, sacred

Devils Tower, which is located in northeastern Wyoming, is sacred to more than twenty Native American tribes, including the Lakota (Sioux), who refer to it as "Bears Lodge." Devils Tower is today a national monument on federal land, but thanks to a 1999 ruling by the United States Court of Appeals for the Tenth Circuit, the Sioux have been awarded the right to worship at the sacred monolith during the holy month of June.

sites have become hotbeds of debate from the different worldviews held by multiple users on federal lands.

Native Americans, Alaska Natives, and Native Hawaiian organizations may be reluctant to share information about sacred sites and practices with non-Natives because of past exploitations and/or traditional practices. It has been very difficult for non-Native Americans to truly understand a land-based religion. Once the public has access to information regarding Native cultural or religious information, the potential for the site to be exploited increases. In Wyoming, the Lakota people have continually had difficulty in gaining access to Devils Tower for religious ceremonies traditionally practiced at this sacred site. Today, serious climbers and other non-Native Americans view this area as an important recreational site. Devils Tower was made even more popular after a portion of the Hollywood film *Close Encounters* was shot there.

The National Park Service attempted to set aside the month of June for Lakota ceremonies and asked other recreational users to respect this time and refrain from climbing and disturbing the Lakota ceremonies. Interestingly, the Black Hills, as well as Devils Tower, were once owned by the Lakotas—under the terms of the Treaty of Fort Laramie—and the tribe has battled to regain title for years. The National Park Service's support of the Lakotas and their use of Devils Tower in June has been challenged in court. The Lakotas continue to use this sacred site and recreational users are asked voluntarily to respect their use of the area at this time. A point of contention with sacred sites in general and Devils Tower specifically is that many non-Native Americans believe this is a way for Native Americans to simply grab land, and there is an atmosphere of distrust with regards to authentic religious use of sacred sites. Related to sacred sites are traditional cultural places (properties).

According to Thomas King and Patricia Parker, "A traditional cultural property is one that can be defined generally as one that is eligible for inclusion in the National Register because of its association with cultural practices or beliefs of a living community that 1) are rooted in that community's history and 2) are important in maintaining the continuing culture identity of the community."[125] Places where traditional events and activities occur may be places eligible for designation as traditional cultural properties as a part of the National Register, which provides a degree of protection for these properties. Some tribes may consider the term *traditional cultural properties* to be inappropriate and prefer to use the term, *traditional cultural places*.[126] Sacred sites can also be designated as traditional cultural properties because they are places where traditional events and activities can occur. When places are designated as traditional cultural properties, they are protected from further development. Damaging a traditional cultural place can impact individuals and communities that may be entitled for protection under the National Environmental Policy Act of 1969. Federal agencies must consider the impact of their activities on traditional cultural properties and those sites eligible for designation as traditional cultural properties.

Bighorn Medicine Wheel

Bighorn Medicine Wheel is a place considered to be the altar for Medicine Mountain, a site considered to be sacred by the Arapaho, Cheyenne, Crow, Lakota, Dakota, Shoshone, Cree, Salish Kootenai, and Blackfeet people, among others. The Bighorn Medicine Wheel is an eighty-foot circle of stones in the Bighorn National Forest on the western peak of Medicine Mountain in north-central Wyoming. In the late 1980s, the U.S. Forest Service wanted to upgrade the access road to this site and build a viewing area for greater public access. Native organizations protested because of the significance of the site, and they were successful in blocking the Forest Service's proposal. Now this site is recognized as a religious site to be protected as a traditional cultural property, or place.

In 1999, Wyoming Sawmills, Inc., a logging company, filed a lawsuit against the Forest Service so that it could harvest wood within the 23,000-acre protected area around the medicine wheel. The company stated that the Forest Service was promoting Native American religious practices by protecting the area. Local Native Americans did not oppose the logging, but rather the transportation of the wood by huge trucks that would damage the environment. The Forest Service argued that they were merely protecting the site for religious use and that their interpretive programs at the medicine wheel are used to explain Native religious practices at these sites to the general public. In December 2001, U.S. District Judge Alan Johnson ruled against Wyoming Sawmills, Inc., and his ruling was upheld by the United States Court of Appeals for the Tenth Circuit in September 2004, after the company filed an appeal in 2002.

National Historic Preservation Act of 1966

The National Historic Preservation Act requires agencies to identify, protect, and manage those sites that are eligible for designation as a traditional cultural property. This law (NHPA) also specifically mentions Native places and religious and cultural sites, and requires consultation with Native Americans, Alaska Natives, and Native Hawaiians. The American Indian Religious Freedom Act requires that agencies respect Native religions, which includes access to sacred sites whether those sacred sites are eligible for the National register or not. Certain locations are held sacred by Native Americans and those sites have cultural importance (plants, animals, deities). Often it is the actual landscape feature that is considered sacred by Native Americans. Mountains, rivers, springs, or waterfalls may be seen as traditional cultural places. These areas tend to be large and hard to define and designate. Traditional cultural properties are not marked because they are natural parts of the landscape. There are exceptions to this in areas such as Pueblo Bonito, which is viewed as a cultural property with traditional significance by Pueblo peoples. The designation for traditional cultural properties is defined under the NHPA. To be eligible as a traditional cultural property, the property must be: important to the community today, important to the community for at least fifty years, must have integrity of condition and purpose (must maintain a degree of the physical significance contributed to its original designation as a culturally significant property and materials and property must maintain the integrity of its purpose), and the property must meet at least one of the four criterion for the National Register.[127]

Traditional Cultural Places

It is difficult to determine the boundaries of a TCP (Traditional Cultural Place) and characteristics that examine how the place is used and why the place is important is critical. Traditional cultural places (properties) and religion must be evaluated

under the First Amendment of the Constitution. It is important to avoid any implications that the United States supports
the religion itself and avoid actions that interfere with the
practice of the religion. Many groups do not distinguish
between religion and culture or the secular and the religious.
Section 304 of the NHPA keeps information about the site
confidential if releasing it could cause invasion of privacy.
When planning an action or project, it is necessary to balance
the need for confidentiality and the need to disclose the effects
of the actions on concerned parties. Public views on a particular traditional cultural property can have an enormous
impact on a site. Shasta Springs Panther Spring was hugely
impacted from visits from the public, mainly "New Age" enthu-
siasts who revere this site largely because of the religious significance attributed to it by the Wintu tribe of California. Visitors
to such sites can have an indirect or direct impact. High places
that have breathtaking views must often remain unimpeded to
maintain the religious nature or use of the site. Spraying plants
can impact traditional gathering for making traditional products, baskets, etc. It is in the dialogue with Native elders and
those with traditional tribal knowledge that an understanding
of how and why the site is important is communicated. It is this
dialogue in which information exchange and listening takes
place so that others can take tribal views into consideration,
when projects, development, or alterations to sites are being
considered.

Again, consultation is the key to identification and protection of sites for modern land use and traditional cultural
places (properties). When project plans do not include Native
tribes from the beginning, it causes great conflict, high costs,
and extensive problems. Those consulting must understand
the perspective of Native Americans and make it a point to listen to and understand from a place of respect. Formal meetings in English or tribal languages is critical. To be respectful
one must actually go into tribal communities, make available

the ability to communicate in a Native language, and be prepared to view sites in the field in order to understand and interpret places. Traditional elders, cultural anthropologists, and sociologists may all be part of a consultation team.

Consultation doesn't always lead to an agreement. Under NHPA Section 106, federal agencies are required to take into account the effects of their actions, consult concerned parties, and give the advisory council a reasonable opportunity to comment. By respecting peoples' concerns about their traditional beliefs and modes of communication, we can protect living traditional cultural places as a part of our environment.

As the world becomes more and more technologically advanced, a major concern is the protection of ideas, symbols, music, etc. The Hopi tribe is in the forefront of addressing cultural preservation and management, and has developed its own cultural preservation office. Its Web site discusses how the Hopis' cultural resources have been abused, appropriated, and violated for many years. They note how "clothing items of ceremonial dancers have been photographed without the dancers' permission and sold," choreography from ceremonial dances has been copied and performed in non-sacred settings, and pictures have been taken and sold with no benefit to the Hopis. The Hopis are not alone in these complaints and there are many tribes who have similar problems and encounters.

In order to sustain tribal culture and spirituality, protection of cultural resources is of the utmost importance to Native peoples. Many would claim that sustainability of both culture and spirituality is connected to the social health and balance of tribal communities. In identifying treatment approaches in tribal communities to address health disparities, both culture and spirituality have played and continue to play a critical role. Many tribal communities most often include cultural components in their approaches when there are funds to initiate treatment programs and educational campaigns to address health disparities and social challenges.

Although there has been little research regarding the effectiveness of cultural approaches, tribal communities continue to develop programs that emphasize some aspect of culture or spirituality in responding to health disparities and social issues within their communities. Although there may be little research in this area, traditional approaches that honor and include balance within traditional Native communities are considered the starting point for many in a decolonization effort to bring back approaches that will protect those who are now victimized within tribal communities today. The challenges and conflicts involved in protecting tribal cultural resources located on tribal, federal, or public lands remains an area of constant conflict and at the same time is an area of critical importance to tribes and the continued cultural and social health of their members.

1500s	Contact with Spanish, French, and English explorers and settlers.
1680	Pueblo Revolt removes Spanish from New Mexico.
1789	Beginning of the treaty making era (ends in 1871).
1805	Tenskwatawa (Shawnee) begins new revitalization movement.
1830	Indian Removal Act passed by Congress.
1831	*Cherokee Nation v. Georgia.*
1832	Congress appropriates funds for health programs that serve Native Americans.
1871	Treaty making comes to an end; Allotment and Assimilation period (1871–1928).
1876	BIA medical division established.
1879	Carlisle Indian School (1879–1918).
1881	Sun Dance outlawed by U.S. government.
1885	Major Crimes Act.
1887	General Allotment Act passed.
1890	Ghost Dance and Wounded Knee Massacre in South Dakota.
1906	Antiquities Act of 1906.
1910	Indian Shaker Church incorporated; BIA is given funding for health-care services.
1918	Native American Church established.
1921	Charles E. Burke, commissioner of Indian Affairs, issues Circular 1662, which prohibits Indian dancing, ceremonies, and religious traditions.
1924	Indian Citizenship Act of 1924.
1928	Meriam Report documents poor Indian health; period of Indian Reorganization (1928–1945).
1934	Indian Reorganization Act passed.
1944	Formation of the National Congress of the American Indian.
1945	Termination Era (1945–1961).

1953 Public Law 280 passed.

1955 Congress transfers the health responsibility from the Bureau of Indian Affairs in Department of the Interior to the U.S. Public Health Services; Indian Health moved to the Department of Health and Human Services.

1956 Relocation Program begins.

1961 Era of Self Determination (1961–Present).

1964 *People v. Woody.*

1966 National Historic Preservation Act (NHPA).

1968 Indian Civil Rights Act of 1968.

1969 National Environmental Policy Act (NEPA).

1970 Taos Pueblos regain Blue Lake.

1971 Alaska Native Claims Settlement Act of 1971.

1972 National Indian Health Board created.

1975 Indian Self-Determination and Education Assistance Act.

1976 Indian Civil Rights Act (ICRA); Indian Health Care Improvement Act.

1978 Indian Child Welfare Act (ICWA); American Indian Religious Freedom Act (AIRFA)

1979 Archaeological Resources Protection Act (ARPA); White Buffalo Calf Woman Society, Inc., the first battered women's shelter in Indian Country is opened and directed by Tillie Black Bear.

1987 National Native American AIDS Prevention Center founded; formation of the Northwest Indian Child Welfare Association (NWICWA), by 1992 NWICWA is renamed the National Indian Child Welfare Association (NICWA).

1990 *Employment Division, Department of Human Resources of Oregon v. Smith*; Native American Graves Protection and Repatriation Act (NAGPRA); Indian Child Protection and Family Violence Protection Act.

1994   Presidential Memorandum: "Government-to-Government Relations with Native American Tribal Governments"; American Indian Religious Freedom Act Amendments; Executive Order 12898, Environmental Justice; Violence Against Women Act is passed.

1995   The Eastern Band of Cherokee Indians open the first Children's Advocacy Center in Indian Country: Heart-to-Heart, Child Advocacy Center in Cherokee, North Carolina.

1996   Executive Order 13007: Indian Sacred Sites; Tribal Law and Policy Institute founded.

1999   Native American Children's Alliance is founded (NACA).

2000   Executive Order 13175: Consultation and Coordination with Indian Tribal governments.

2001   *Killing Us Quietly*, first book on Native Americans and HIV/AIDS, published.

2003   Civil Rights Report published, *Quiet Crisis: Federal Funding and Unmet Needs in Indian Country.*

2004   *United States v. Lara.*

Notes

Chapter 1:
Native American Social Issues in the Twenty-First Century

1 Helen Exley, *In beauty may I walk . . . Words of Peace and Wisdom By Native Americans* (New York: Exley Publishing, 1997).

2 Oren Lyons, *Native Wisdom*, ed. Joseph Bruchac (New York: Harper/San Francisco Publishers, 1995), 30. Reprint Oregon: Harvey Arden and Steve Wall, eds. *Wisdom Keepers*, copyright, 1990.

Chapter 2:
Native American Health

3 "Frist, Landrieu Unveil Health Disparities Bill," Press Release, Bill Frist, M.D. website, *www.frist.senate.gov*. Accessed 2/24/05.

4 Thornton Russell, *American Indian Holocaust and Survival: A Population History since 1492* (Norman, Okla.: University of Oklahoma Press, 1987), 133.

5 Jennie R. Joe, "The Rationing of Healthcare and Health Disparity for the American Indians/Alaska Natives," In *Unequal Treatment: Confronting Racial and Ethnic Disparities in Healthcare*, ed. Brian D. Smedley, Adrienne Y. Stith, and Alan R. Nelson, 528–551 (Washington, D.C.: The National Academies Press, 2003), 530–31.

6 Brett Lee Shelton, "Legal and Historical Roots of Health Care for American Indians and Alaska Natives in the United States," *Kaiser Family Foundation Issue Brief*, February 2004, 6.

7 Ibid., 7.

8 Irene Vernon, *Killing Us Quietly: Native Americans and HIV/AIDS* (Lincoln, Nebr.: University of Nebraska Press, 2001), 2.

9 U.S. Commission on Civil Rights. *A Quiet Crisis: Federal Funding and Unmet Needs in Indian Country* (Washington, D.C.: U.S. Commission on Civil Rights, July 2003), 47.

10 Ibid., 34.

11 David H. Getches, Charles F. Wilkinson, and Robert A. Williams, Jr., *Federal Indian Law; Cases and Materials*, 5th Edition (St Paul, Minn.: Thomson/West, 2005,) 18.; Cancer Mortality Among American Indians and Alaska Natives—United States, 1994–1998.

CDC MMWR Weekly, August 1, 2003/52 (30); 704–707.

12 Joe, "The Rationing of Healthcare and Health Disparity for the American Indians/Alaska Natives," 549.

13 U.S. Commission on Civil Rights. *A Quiet Crisis:*, 43.

14 Ibid., X.

15 Ibid., 46.

16 U.S. Census Bureau, *The American Indian and Alaska Native Population: 2000*, February 2002, 1.

17 Ibid., 3.

18 Ibid., 4.

19 U.S. Department of Health and Human Services, Indian Health Service, FY 2004 Budget Request, Justification of Estimates for Appropriations Committees: *http://www.ihs.gov/ AdminMngrResources/Budget/FY_2004,_Budfg et_Justification.asp*, 93.

20 Office of Statistics and Programming, National Center for Injury Prevention and Control, *CDC* "10 Leading Causes of Death; American Indian and Alaska Natives, Both Sexes, 1999–2000."

21 Ibid; Gretchen Ehrsam Day and Anne P. Lanier, *Alaska Native Mortality, 1979–1998 Public Health Report*, November–December 2003, 8.

22 CDC/NCHS and the American Heart Association, American Indians/Alaska Natives and Cardiovascular Diseases; Biostatistical Fact Sheet—Populations, 2002, 2–3.

23 *Alaska Native Mortality, 1979–1998 Public Health Report*, 3.

24 CDC, Cancer Mortality among American Indians and Alaska Natives—United States, 1994–1998, *MMWR Weekly*, August 1, 2003, 52(30); 704–707.

25 Ibid.

26 Ibid. CDC Media Relations, "Risk Factors for Chronic Disease and Injury Vary Greatly by Region and Sex among American Indians and Alaska Natives," 2000: *http://www.cdc.gov/od/oc/media/pressrel/r2k020 4.htm*.

27 Ibid.

28 "10 Leading Causes of Death; American Indian and Alaska Natives, Both Sexes, 1999–2000."

Notes

29 "10 Leading Causes of Death; American Indian and Alaska Natives, Both Sexes, 1999–2000.; CDC Media Relations, "Risk Factors for Chronic Disease and Injury Vary Greatly by Region and Sex Among American Indians and Alaska Natives," 2000.; *CDC MMWR Weekly*, August 1, 2003/52 (30); 697–701.

30 "Risk Factors for Chronic Disease and Injury Vary Greatly by Region and Sex among American Indians and Alaska Natives," 2000.

31 Philip May, "Alcohol-Related Motor Vehicle Fatalities on and around the New Mexico Portion of the Navajo Indian Reservation: A Baseline Study of the Pattern 1982–1986," In *Alcohol Use among American Indians and Alaska Natives: Multiple Perspectives on a Complex Problem*, ed. Patricia D. Mail, Suzanne Heurtin-Roberts, Susan E. Martin, and Jan Howard (Bethesda, Md.: U.S. Department of Health and Human Services, 2002), 411–428.

32 Ibid., 424.

33 Ibid., 423–424.

34 "10 Leading Causes of Death; American Indian and Alaska Natives, Both Sexes, 1999–2000.; *CDC MMWR Weekly*, August 1, 2003/52 (30); 697–701.; American Academy of Pediatrics, The Prevention of Unintentional Injury among American Indian and Alaska Native Children: A Subject Review (RE9908), Policy Statement, Pediatrics, vol. 104, no. 6, 1999, 1397–1399.

35 Ibid.

36 Fred Beauvais, Pamela Jumper-Thurman, and Barbara Plested, "Prevention of Alcohol and Other Drug Abuse among Indian Adolescents: An Examination of Current Assumptions," In *Alcohol Use among American Indians and Alaska Natives: Multiple Perspectives on a Complex Problem*, ed. Patricia D. Mail, Suzanne Heurtin-Roberts, Susan E. Martin, and Jan Howard (Bethesda, Md.: U.S. Department of Health and Human Services, 2002), 198.

37 Patricia D. Mail, "Multiple Perspectives on Alcohol and the American Indian, In *Alcohol Use among American Indians and Alaska Natives: Multiple Perspectives on a Complex Problem*, ed. Patricia D. Mail, Suzanne

Heurtin-Roberts, Susan E. Martin, and Jan Howard, (Bethesda, Md.: U.S. Department of Health and Human Services, 2002).

38 May, "Alcohol-Related Motor Vehicle Fatalities," 421–423.

39 F.N. Ferguson, "Navajo Drinking: Some Tentative Hypothesis," *Human Organization* 27: 159–167, 1968.

40 May, "Alcohol-Related Motor Vehicle Fatalities," 422.

41 Ibid.; Philip May and M.B. Smith, "Some Navajo Indian Opinions about Alcohol Abuse and Prohibition: A Survey and Recommendations for Policy," *J Stud Alcohol* 49(4):324–334, 1988.

42 Ibid., 424–425.

43 Ibid., 421–424.

44 Ibid., 422–424.

45 CDC Diabetes Prevalence among American Indians and Alaska Natives and the Overall Population—United States, 1994–2002. *CDC MMWR Weekly*, August 1, 2003/52 (30); 702–704.

46 CDC, Publications and Products: Fact Sheet, "Trends in Diabetes Prevalence among American Indian and Alaska Native Children, Adolescents, and Young Adults: 1990–1998: *http://www.cdc.gov/diabetes/pubs/factsheets/aian.htmn.*

47 Ibid.

48 CDC Diabetes Prevalence among American Indians and Alaska Natives and the Overall Population—United States, 1994–2002. *CDC MMWR Weekly*, August 1, 2003/52 (30); 702–704.

49 U.S. Commission on Civil Rights. *A Quiet Crisis: Federal Funding and Unmet Needs in Indian Country* (Washington, D.C.: U.S. Commission on Civil Rights, July 2003), 47.

50 CDC Diabetes Prevalence among American Indians and Alaska Natives and the Overall Population—United States, 1994–2002. *CDC MMWR Weekly*, August 1, 2003/52 (30); 702–704; CDC, Publications and Products: Fact Sheet, "Trends in Diabetes Prevalence among American Indian and Alaska Native Children, Adolescents, and Young Adults— 1990–1998.

51 U.S. Commission on Civil Rights. *A Quiet Crisis: Federal Funding and Unmet Needs in*

Notes

Indian Country (Washington, D.C.: U.S. Commission on Civil Rights, July 2003), 47.

52 Joe, "The Rationing of Healthcare and Health Disparity," 530.

53 Amanda Smith Barush, *Foundations of Social Policy: Social Justice, Public Programs, and the Social Work Profession* (Belmont, Calif.: Thomson Brooks/Cole, 2002)109–112.; U.S. Census Bureau, Poverty in the United States: 2001, Current Population Reports, September, 2002, 7.; U.S. Commission on Civil Rights. *A Quiet Crisis: Federal Funding and Unmet Needs in Indian Country* (Washington, D.C.: U.S. Commission on Civil Rights, July 2003), 8.

54 U.S. Commission on Civil Rights. *A Quiet Crisis: Federal Funding and Unmet Needs in Indian Country* (Washington: U.S. Commission on Civil Rights, July 2003), 8–9; U.S. Census Bureau, "Sex by Employment Status for the Population 16 Years and over (American Indian and Alaska Native Alone)": *www.factfinder.census.gov/serlet/DTTable?ts=75 2105180875.*

55 Michael Bird, "Health Indigenous People: Recommendations for the Next Generation," *American Journal of Public Health*, 92 (September 2002), 1392.

Chapter 3:
Native Americans and HIV/AIDS

56 Joseph Dalaker, *Poverty in the United States: 2000*, U.S. Department of Commerce (U.S. Census Bureau: U.S. Government Publication, 2001), 6.

57 Paul Spicer and Fred Beauvais, "Re-Examining Alcohol Problems among American Indian Communities" *Alcoholism: Clinical & Experimental Research*, November 13, 2003.

Chapter 4:
Violence against Native American Women and Children

58 Ward Churchill, *Perversions of Justice: Indigenous Peoples and AngloAmerican Law* (San Francisco, Calif.: City Light Books, 2003), 12–13, 153; David H. Getches, Charles F. Wilkinson, and Robert A. Williams, Jr. Cases and Materials on Federal Indian Law, 4th Edition (St. Paul, Minn.: West Group, 1998), 4–5; David E. Wilkins, *American Indian*

Politics and the American Political System (New York: Rowman & Littlefield Publishers, Inc., 2002), 93.

59 Bonnie Duran, Eduardo Duran, and Maria Yellow Horse Brave Heart, "Native Americans and the Trauma of History," In *Studying Native America: Problem and Prospects*, ed., Russell Thornton (Madison, Wisc.: University of Wisconsin Press, 1998), 61.

60 Ibid., 61–66.

61 Jorge Noriega, "American Indian Education in the United States: Indoctrination for Subordination to Colonialism," in *The State of Native America: Genocide, Colonization and Resistance*, ed., M. Annette Jaimes (Boston, Mass.: South End Press, 1992), 380.

62 Ibid., 380–384.

63 Robert Bensen, ed., *Children of the Dragonfly: Native American Voices on Child Custody and Education* (Tucson, Ariz.: University of Arizona Press, 2001), 3–18.; Charlene LaPointe, "Boarding Schools Teach Violence," *Plainswoman*, 10: 3–4.

64 Duran, Duran, and Yellow Horse Brave Heart, "Native Americans and the Trauma of History," 62–67.

65 Theda Perdue, *Sifters: Native American Women's Lives* (New York: Oxford University Press, 2001), 4, 31, 120.

66 Ibid., 4.

67 Ibid., 49, 93, 94, 120.

68 M. Annette Jaimes and Theresa Halsey, "American Indian Women at the Center of Indigenous Resistance in Contemporary North America," in *The State of Native America: Genocide, Colonization and Resistance*, ed. M. Annette Jaimes (Boston, Mass.: South End Press, 1992), 311; Personal communication with Theresa Halsey, August 2004.

69 Karen Artichoker, 8th National Indian Nations conference. Personal communication, 2002.

70 Karen Artichoker and Marlin Mousseau, "Violence and the American Indian Woman," *Center for Prevention of Sexual and Domestic Violence Newsletter*, 5, 4: 5–7.

71 Sherry Hamby, "The Importance of Community in a Feminist Analysis of Domestic Violence among American Indians," *American Journal of Community Psychology* 28, 5: 649–669.

72 Lawrence Greenfield and Steven Smith, "American Indians and Crime," U.S. Department of Justice, Office of Justice Programs, Bureau of Justice Statistics, 1999, Washington, D.C.

73 Ibid.; Kathleen A. Earle and Amanda Cross, *Child Abuse and Neglect among American Indian/Alaska Native Children: An Analysis of Existing Data* (Seattle, Wash.: Casey Family Programs, 2001), 7.

74 Patricia Tjaden and Nancy Thoennes, "Full Report of the Prevalence, Incidence, and Consequences of Violence against Women: Findings from the National Violence against Women Survey," National Institute of Justice and Center for Disease Control, 2000, Washington, D.C., 35, 39; Karina L. Walters and Jane M. Simone, "Reconceptualizing Native Women's Health: An Indigenist Stress-Coping Model," *American Journal of Public Health*, 2002, vol. 92, no. 4., 522.

75 Jeffrey D. Edelson and Michael D. Frank, "Rural Interventions in Women Battering: One State's Strategies," Families in Society: *The Journal of Contemporary Human Services* 72: 543–551.

76 Lawrence Greenfield and Steven Smith, "American Indians and Crime," U.S. Department of Justice, Office of Justice Programs, Bureau of Justice Statistics, 2004, Washington, D.C.

77 Ibid.

78 Patricia Tjaden and Nancy Thoennes, "Research in Brief: Prevalence, Incidence, and Consequences of Violence against Women: Findings from the National Violence against Women Survey," National Institute of Justice and Center for Disease Control, 1998, Washington, D.C., 35, 39.

79 L.J. Wallace, Alice D. David, Kenneth E. Calhoun, Joan O'Neil Powell, and Stephen P. James, *Homicide and Suicide among Native Americans, 1979–1992* (Atlanta, Ga.: Centers for Disease Control and Prevention, National Center for Injury Prevention and Control. Violence Surveillance Summary Series, No. 2, 1996).

80 Greenfield and Smith, "American Indians and Crime."

81 Tjaden and Thoennes, "Research in Brief:

Prevalence, Incidence, and Consequences of Violence against Women: Findings from the National Violence Against Women Survey."

82 Karen Artichoker, 8th National Indian Nations Conference, Personal Communication, 2002; Sherry Hamby, "The Importance of Community in a Feminist Analysis of Domestic Violence among American Indians" *American Journal of Community Psychology* 28, 5: 649–669.

83 National Center for Injury and Control, "American Indian/Alaska Natives and Intimate partner Violence," 2000: *www.cdc.gov.ncipc.dv.*

84 Greenfield and Smith, "American Indians and Crime."

85 Laura A. Williams, "Family Violence and American Indians/Alaska Natives: A Report to the Indian Health Service Office of Women's Health, Executive Summary."

86 Greenfield and Smith, "American Indians and Crime."

87 Patricia D. Mail and Patricia Silk Walker, "Alcohol in the Lives of Indian Women," in *Alcohol Use among American Indians and Alaska Natives: Multiple Perspectives on a Complex Problem*, ed. Patricia D. Mail, Suzanne Heurtin-Roberts, Susan E. Martin, and Jan Howard (Bethesda, Md.: U.S. Department of Health and Human Services, 2002), 242.

88 Ibid., 247.

89 Ibid., 249.

90 Ibid.

91 "10 Leading Causes of Death; American Indian and Alaska Natives, Both Sexes, 1999–2000."

92 Mail and Walker, "Alcohol in the Lives of Indian Women," 251.

93 Jeffrey D. Edelson and Michael D. Frank, "Rural Interventions in Women Battering: One State's Strategies," *Families in Society: The Journal of Contemporary Human Services* 72: 543–551.

94 Sarah Deer, Joseph Flies-Away, Carrie Garrow, Elton Naswood, and Diane Payne, *Victim Services Promising Practices in Indian Country* (Washington, D.C.: Office for Victims of Crime, 2004), 37–39.

95 Duran, Duran, and Yellow Horse Brave Heart,

"Native Americans and the Trauma of History," 61–66.

96 M.R. Petit and A.A. Curtis, *Child Abuse and Neglect: A Look at the States* (Washington, D.C.: CWLA Press, 1997).

97 Kathleen A. Earle and Amanda Cross, *Child Abuse and Neglect among American Indian/Alaska Native Children: An Analysis of Existing Data* (Seattle, Wash.: Casey Family Programs, 2001), 58–60.

98 Roe Bubar, Unpublished Paper, "Native Language Use in Child Sexual Abuse Investigations," 2002.

99 Ibid.

100 Paul M. Ong, Hyun-Gun Sung and Julia Heintz-Mackoff, *American Indian Children in Los Angeles, California & the U.S.* (Los Angeles, Calif.: UCLA Ralph & Goldy Lewis Center for Regional Policy Studies, 2004), 1–7.

101 Petit and Curtis, *Child Abuse and Neglect: A Look at the States*.

102 Greenfield and Smith, "American Indians and Crime."

103 Ibid.

104 Eidell Wasserman, Roe Bubar, and Teresa Cain, *Children's Advocacy Centers in Indian Country* (Norman, Okla.: University of Oklahoma Health Services and Office for Victims of Crime, 2000).

105 Kathleen Coulborn Faller, "Child Sexual Abuse: A Case Study in Community Collaboration," *Child Abuse & Neglect*, vol. 24, no. 9, 1223.

106 Ibid., 1223.

107 Roe Bubar, *The Native American Children's Alliance Report on Children's Advocacy Centers & Select Multidisciplinary Teams in Indian Country and Alaska Native Communities* (Albuquerque, N.M.: Native American Children's Alliance, 2003), 3.

Chapter 5:
Native American Sacred and Ceremony

108 J. Niles Hubbard, *An Account of Sa-Go-Ye-Wat-Ha or Red Jacket and His People, 1750–1830* (New York: Lenox Hill, 1886, reprint New York: Burt Franklin, 1972), 235.

109 Ann Nugent, *Schooling of the Lummi Indians between 1855–1956* (Lincoln, Nebr.: University of Nebraska Press, 1979), 161.

Chapter 6:
Cultural Resources

110 Andrew Gulliford, *Sacred Objects and Sacred Places; Preserving Tribal Traditions* (Boulder, Colo.: University of Colorado Press, 2000), 1.

111 Thomas F. King, *Cultural Resource Laws & Practice; An Introductory Guide* (New York: Alta Mira Press, 1998), 267.

112 Ibid., 98.

113 Native American Graves Protection and Repatriation Act, 25 U.S.C. §§ 3001–3013, 1990 (Supp. 1991).

114 *Cherokee Nation v. Georgia*, 30 U.S. (5 Pet.) 1, 1831.

115 William J. Clinton, Government-to-Government Relationship, Memorandum for the Heads of Executive Departments and Agencies, Memorandum of April 29, 1994 [59 FR 22951], Washington, D.C.

116 Ibid.

117 William J. Clinton, Indian Sacred Sites, Executive Order 13007 of May 24, 1996, [61FR 26771], Washington, D.C.

118 American Indian Religious Freedom Act, Pub.L. 95-341, 42 U.S.C.A. § 1996.

119 Gulliford, *Sacred Objects and Sacred Places; Preserving Tribal Traditions*, 160.

120 Antiquities Act of 1906, 16, U.S.C. 431-433.

121 Native American Graves Protection and Repatriation Act, 25 U.S.C. §§ 3001-3013, 1990 (Supp. 1991).

122 Roger C. Echo-Hawk and Walter R. Echo-Hawk, *Battlefields and Burial Grounds: The Indian Struggle to Protect Ancestral Graves in the United States* (Minneapolis, Minn.: Lerner Publications Company, 1994), 20–21.

123 *Through the Generations: Traditional Cultural Properties*, Produced by U.S. Department of the Interior, National Park Service, U.S. Department of Agriculture, Natural Resources Conservation Service and Advisory Council on Historic Preservation. Video. 20 min.

124 Ibid.

125 Patricia Parker and Thomas F. King, National Register Bulletin #38, "Guidelines

for Evaluating and Documenting Traditional
Cultural Properties," 1.

126 Gulliford, *Sacred Objects and Sacred Places;
Preserving Tribal Traditions*, 103.

127 Patrick W. Andrus, National Register Criteria
for Evaluation, 36 CFR Part 60, 1990.

American Academy of Pediatrics. "The Prevention of Unintentional Injury among American Indian and Alaska Native Children: A Subject Review (RE9908), Policy Statement," *Pediatrics*, 104, (6), (1999): 1397–1399.

American Indian Religious Freedom Act, Public Law 95-341, 42 U.S.C.A. § 1996.

Andrus, Patrick. W. National Register Criteria for Evaluation, 36 CFR Part 60, 1990.

Antiquities Act of 1906, 16, U.S.C. 431–433.

Artichoker, Karen, and Marlin Mousseau. "Violence and the American Indian Woman." *Center for Prevention of Sexual and Domestic Violence Newsletter*, 5, 4: 5–7.

Barush, Amanda. *Foundations of Social Policy: Social Justice, Public Programs, and the Social Work Profession.* Belmont, Calif.: Thomson Brooks/Cole, 2002.

Beauvais, Fred, Pamela Jumper-Thurman, and Barbara Plested. "Prevention of Alcohol and Other Drug Abuse among Indian Adolescents: An Examination of Current Assumptions." In *Alcohol Use among American Indians and Alaska Natives: Multiple Perspectives on a Complex Problem*, edited by Patricia D. Mail, Suzanne Heurtin-Roberts, Susan E. Martin, and Jan Howard. Bethesda, Md.: U.S. Department of Health and Human Services, 2002.

Bensen, Robert, ed. *Children of the Dragonfly: Native American Voices on Child Custody and Education.* Tucson, Ariz.: University of Arizona Press, 2001.

Bird, Michael. "Health Indigenous People: Recommendations for the Next Generation. *American Journal of Public Health* 92 (September 2002): 1391–92.

Bubar, Roe. *Interviewing Native Children in Child Sexual Abuse Cases.* Norman, Okla.: University of Oklahoma Health Services and Office for Victims of Crime, 2000.

———. "The Native American Children's Alliance's Report on Children's Advocacy Centers & Select Multidisciplinary Teams in Indian Country and Alaska Native Communities." Albuquerque, N.M.: Native American Children's Alliance, 2003.

———. Unpublished Paper, Native Language Use in Child Sexual Abuse Investigations, 2002.

CDC. "Cancer Mortality among American Indians and Alaska Natives—United States, 1994–1998." *CDC MMWR Weekly*, August 1, 2003/52 (30).

————. "Diabetes Prevalence among American Indians and Alaska Native Americans and the Overall Population—United States, 1994–2002." *CDC MMWR Weekly*, August 1, 2003/52 (30).

————. "Injury Mortality among American Indian and Alaska Native Children and Youth—United States, 1989–1998," *CDC MMWR Weekly*, August 1, 2003/52 (30).

CDC/NCHS and the American Heart Association. "American Indians/Alaska Natives and Cardiovascular Diseases; Biostatistical Fact Sheet—Populations," 2002.

CDC. Media Relations, "Risk Factors for Chronic Disease and Injury Vary Greatly by Region and Sex among American Indians and Alaska Native Americans." 2000. *http://www.cdc.gov/od/oc/media/pressrel/r2k0204.htm*.

————. Publications and Products: Fact Sheet, "Trends in Diabetes Prevalence among American Indian and Alaska Native Children, Adolescents, and Young Adults—1990–1998." *http://www.cdc.gov/diabetes/pubs/factsheets/aian.htm*.

Cherokee Nation v. Georgia, 30 U.S. (5 Pet.) 1, 1831.

Churchill, Ward. *Perversions of Justice: Indigenous Peoples and AngloAmerican Law*. San Francisco, Calif.: City Light Books, 2003.

Clinton, William, J. "Government-to-Government Relationship, Memorandum for the Heads of Executive Departments and Agencies," Memorandum of April 29, 1994 [59 FR 22951], Washington, D.C.

————. "Indian Sacred Sites," Executive Order 13007 of May 24, 1996, [61FR 26771], Washington, D.C..

Dalaker, Joseph. *Poverty in the United States: 2000*. U.S. Department of Commerce, U.S. Census Bureau: U.S. Government Publication, 2001.

Day, Gretchen Ehrsam, and Anne P. Lanier. *Alaska Native Mortality, 1979–1998 Public Health Report*, November–December 2003.

Deer, Sarah, Joseph Flies-Away, Carrie Garrow, Elton Naswood, and Diane Payne. *Victim Services Promising Practices in Indian Country*. Washington, D.C.: Office for Victims of Crime, 2004.

Deloria, Vine. *Custer Died for Your Sins: An Indian Manifesto*. New York: Avon Books, 1969.

————. *God is Red: A Native View of Religion*. New York: Fulcrum Press,

2003, Gossett, 1972.

Duran, Bonnie, Eduardo Duran, and Maria Yellow Horse Brave Heart. "Native Americans and the Trauma of History." In *Studying Native America: Problem and Prospects,* edited by Russell Thornton, Madison, Wisc.: University of Wisconsin Press, 1998.

Earle, Kathleen A., and Amanda Cross. *Child Abuse and Neglect among American Indian/Alaska Native Children: An Analysis of Existing Data.* Seattle, Wash.: Casey Family Programs, 2001.

Echo-Hawk, Roger, C., and Walter R. Echo-Hawk. *Battlefields and Burial Grounds: The Indian Struggle to Protect Ancestral Graves in the United States.* Minneapolis, Minn.: Lerner Publications Company, 1994.

Edelson, Jeffrey, L., and Michael D. Frank. "Rural Interventions in Women Battering: One State's Strategies." Families in Society: *The Journal of Contemporary Human Services* 72: 543–551.

Exley, Helen. *In Beauty May I Walk. . .Words of Peace and Wisdom by Native Americans.* New York: Exley Publishing, 1997.

Faller, Kathleen Coulborn. "Child Sexual Abuse: A Case Study in Community Collaboration." *Child Abuse & Neglect.* Vol. 24, No. 9, 1223.

Ferguson, F.N. "Navajo Drinking: Some Tentative Hypothesis." *Human Organization* 27: 159–167, 1968.

"Frist, Landrieu Unveil Health Disparities Bill," Press Release, Bill Frist, M.D. website: *http://frist.senate.gov.*

Getches, David H., Charles F. Wilkinson, and Robert A. Williams, Jr. *Federal Indian Law; Cases and Materials,* 5th Edition, St Paul, Minn.: Thomson/West, 2005.

Greenfield, Lawrence, and Steven Smith. "American Indians and Crime," U.S. Department of Justice, Office of Justice Programs, Bureau of Justice Statistics, 1999. Washington, D.C.

———. "American Indians and Crime." U.S. Department of Justice, Office of Justice Programs, Bureau of Justice Statistics, 2004. Washington, D.C.

Gulliford, Andrew. *Sacred Objects and Sacred Places; Preserving Tribal Traditions.* Boulder, Colo.: University of Colorado Press, 2000.

Hamby, Sherry. "The Importance of Community in a Feminist Analysis of Domestic Violence Among American Indians." *American Journal of Community Psychology* 28, 5: 649–669.

Hubbard, J. Niles. *An Account of Sa-Go-Ye-Wat-Ha or Red Jacket and His People, 1750–1830.* New York: Lenox Hill, 1886, reprint New York: Burt Franklin, 1972.

Jaimes, M. Annette, and Theresa Halsey. "American Indian Women at the Center of Indigenous Resistance in Contemporary North America." In *The State of Native America: Genocide, Colonization and Resistance*, edited by M. Annette Jaimes. Boston, Mass.: South End Press, 1992.

Joe, Jennie R. "The Rationing of Healthcare and Health Disparity for the American Indians/Alaska Natives." In *Unequal Treatment: Confronting Racial and Ethnic Disparities in Healthcare*, edited by Brian D. Smedley, Adrienne Y. Stith, and Alan R. Nelson. Washington, D.C.: The National Academies Press, 2003.

King, Thomas, F. *Cultural Resource Laws & Practice: An Introductory Guide.* New York: Alta Mira Press, 1998.

LaPointe, Charlene. "Boarding Schools Teach Violence." *Plainswoman*, 10: 3–4.

Lyons, Oren. *Native Wisdom*, edited by Joseph Bruchac. New York: Harper/San Francisco, 1995. Reprint Oregon: Harvey Arden and Steve Wall editors, *Wisdom Keepers*, copyright, 1990.

Mail, Patricia, D., and Patricia Silk Walker. "Alcohol in the Lives of Indian Women." In *Alcohol Use among American Indians and Alaska Natives: Multiple Perspectives on a Complex Problem*, edited by Patricia D. Mail, Suzanne Heurtin-Roberts, Susan E. Martin, and Jan Howard. Bethesda, Md.: U.S. Department of Health and Human Services, 2002.

May, Philip. "Alcohol-Related Motor Vehicle Fatalities on and around the New Mexico Portion of the Navajo Indian Reservation: A Baseline Study of the Pattern 1982–1986." In *Alcohol Use among American Indians and Alaska Native Americans: Multiple Perspectives on a Complex Problem*, edited by Patricia D. Mail, Suzanne Heurtin-Roberts, Susan E. Martin, and Jan Howard, 411–428. Bethesda, Md.: U.S. Department of Health and Human Services, 2002.

National Center for Injury and Control. "American Indian/Alaska Natives and Intimate Partner Violence," 2000. *www.cdc.gov.ncipc.dv.*

Native American Graves Protection and Repatriation Act, 25 U.S.C. §§ 3001-3013, 1990. Supp. 1991.

Noriega, Jorge. "American Indian Education in the United States: Indoctrination for Subordination to Colonialism." In *The State of Native America: Genocide, Colonization and Resistance*, edited by M. Annette Jaimes, 371–402. Boston, Mass.: South End Press, 1992.

Nugent, Ann. *Schooling of the Lummi Indians between 1855–1956*. Lincoln Nebr.: University of Nebraska Press, 1979.

Office of Statistics and Programming, National Center for Injury Prevention and Control, *CDC "10 Leading Causes of Death; American Indian and Alaska Natives, Both Sexes, 1999–2000*.

Ong, Paul M., Hyun-Gun Sung, and Julia Heintz-Mackoff. *American Indian Children in Los Angeles, California & the U.S.* Los Angeles, Calif.: UCLA Ralph & Goldy Lewis Center for Regional Policy Studies, 2004.

Parker, Patricia, and Thomas F. King. National Register Bulletin #38, "Guidelines for Evaluating and Documenting Traditional Cultural Properties."

Petit, Michael, R., and Patrick A. Curtis. *Child Abuse and Neglect: A Look at the States*. Washington, D.C.: CWLA Press, 1997.

Perdue, Theda. *Sifters: Native American Women's Lives*. New York: Oxford University Press, 2001.

Personal communication with Karen Artichoker, 8th National Indian Nations Conference, 2002.

Personal communication with Theresa Halsey, August 2004.

Russell, Thornton. *American Indian Holocaust and Survival: A Population History since 1492*. Norman, Okla.: University of Oklahoma Press, 1987.

Shelton, Brett Lee. "Legal and Historical Roots of Health Care for American Indians and Alaska Natives in the United States." Kaiser Family Foundation Issue Brief, February 2004.

Spicer, Paul, and Fred Beauvais. "Re-examining Alcohol Problems among American Indian Communities." *Alcoholism: Clinical & Experimental Research*, November 13, 2003.

Through the Generations: Traditional Cultural Properties. Produced by U.S. Department of the Interior, National Park Service, U.S. Department of Agriculture, Natural Resources Conservation Service and Advisory Council on Historic Preservation. Video. 20 min.

Tjaden, Patricia, and Nancy Thoennes. "Full Report of the Prevalence, Incidence, and Consequences of Violence against Women: Findings from the National Violence Against Women Survey," National Institute of Justice and Center for Disease Control, 2000. Washington, D.C.

U.S. Census Bureau. "Sex by Employment Status for the Population 16 Years and Over (American Indian and Alaska Natives Alone)." *www.factfinder.census.gov/serlet/DTTable?ts=752105180875.*

———. "The American Indian and Alaska Native Population: 2000." February, 2002.

U.S. Commission on Civil Rights. "A Quiet Crisis: Federal Funding and Unmet Needs in Indian Country." Washington, D.C: U.S. Commission on Civil Rights, 2003.

U.S. Department of Health and Human Services, Indian Health Service, FY 2004 Budget Request, Justification of Estimates for Appropriations Committees: *http://www.ihs.gov/ AdminMngrResources/Budget/FY_2004,_Budfget_Justification.asp.*

Vernon, Irene. "Indian Religious Freedom in the United States: 1933–1991." MA Thesis, University of New Mexico, 1991.

———. *Killing Us Quietly: Native Americans and HIV/AIDS.* Lincoln, Nebr.: University of Nebraska Press, 2001.

———, and Bubar, Roe. "Child Sexual Abuse and HIV/AIDS in Indian Country." *Wicazo Sa Review*, [Special edition] 16, (2002): 47–63.

Wallace, L.J. David, Alice D. David, Kenneth E. Calhoun, Joan O'Neil Powell, and Stephen P. James. *Homicide and Suicide among Native Americans, 1979–1992.* Atlanta, Ga.: Centers for Disease Control and Prevention, National Center for Injury Prevention and Control. Violence Surveillance Summary Series, No. 2, 1996.

Walters, Karina, L. and Jane M. Simone. "Reconceptualizing Native Women's Health: An Indigenist Stress-Coping Model." *American Journal of Public Health*, 2002, vol. 92, no. 4.

Wasserman, Eidell, Roe Bubar, and Teresa Cain. *Children's Advocacy Centers in Indian Country.* Norman, Okla.: University of Oklahoma Health Services and Office for Victims of Crime, 2000.

Wilkins, David, E. *American Indian Politics and the American Political System.* New York: Rowman & Littlefield Publishers, Inc., 2002.

Williams, Laura, A. "Family Violence and American Indians/Alaska Native Americans: A Report to the Indian Health Service Office of Women's Health, Executive Summary."

Books/Articles

Bensen, Robert. *Children of the Dragonfly: Native American Voices on Child Custody and Education.* Tucson, Ariz.: University of Arizona Press, 2001.

Bird, Michael, ed. *Eliminating Health Disparities: Conversations with American Indians and Alaska Native Americans.* Santa Cruz, Calif.: ETR Associates, 2002.

Bubar, Roe. *Basic Guidelines for Forensic Interviews in Child Sexual Abuse Cases in Indian Country and Alaska Native Communities.* Santa Monica, Calif.: Tribal Law and Policy, 2002 reprinted, 2004.

Echo-Hawk, Roger, and W. R. Echo-Hawk. *Battlefields and Burial Grounds: The Indian Struggle to Protect Ancestral Graves in the United States.* Minneapolis, Minn.: Lerner Publications Company, 1994.

Gulliford, Andrew. *Sacred Objects and Sacred Places: Preserving Tribal Traditions.* Boulder, Colo.: University of Colorado Press, 2000.

Joe, Jennie R. "The Rationing of Healthcare and Health Disparity for the American Indians/Alaska Natives." In *Unequal Treatment: Confronting Racial and Ethnic Disparities in Healthcare*, edited by Brian D. Smedley, Adrienne Y. Stith, and Alan R. Nelson. Washington, D.C.: The National Academies Press, 2003.

Mihesuah, Devon A., ed. *Repatriation Reader: Who Owns American Indian Remains?* Lincoln, Nebr.: University of Nebraska Press, 2000.

Perdue, Theda. *Sifters: Native American Women's Lives.* New York: Oxford University Press, 2001.

Rhoades, Everett R., ed. *American Indian Health: Innovations in Health Care, Promotion, and Policy.* Baltimore, Md.: The Johns Hopkins University Press, 2000.

Smedley, Brian, et al. *Unequal Treatment: Confronting Racial and Ethnic Disparities in Health Care.* Washington, D.C.: The National Academies Press, 2003.

Tjaden, Patricia, and Nancy Thoennes. *Research in Brief: Prevalence, Incidence and Consequences of Violence against Women Survey.* Washington D.C.: National Institute of Justice, Centers for Disease Control and Prevention, 1998.

Treat, James, ed. *Christian and Native: Indigenous Voices on Religious Identity in the United States and Canada.* New York: Routledge, 1996.

U.S. Census Bureau. "Poverty in the United States: 2001, Current Population Reports." September, 2002.

U.S. Commission on Civil Rights. *A Quiet Crisis: Federal Funding and Unmet Needs in Indian Country*. Washington, D.C: U.S. Commission on Civil Rights, 2003.

U.S. Department of Justice. *American Indians and Crime*. Washington D.C.: Office of Justice Programs, Bureau of Justice Statistics, U.S. Government Printing, 1999.

Vernon, Irene S. *Killing Us Quietly: Native Americans and HIV/AIDS*. Lincoln, Nebr.: University of Nebraska Press, 2001.

Deloria, Vine. *God is Red: A Native View of Religion*. New York: Fulcrum Press, 2003.

Wallace, L.J., Alice D. David, Kenneth E. Calhoun, Joan O'Neil Powell, and Stephen P. James. *Homicide and Suicide among Native Americans, 1979–1992*. Atlanta, Ga.: Centers for Disease Control and Prevention, Violence Surveillance Summary Series, No.2. U.S. Government Publication, 1996.

Websites

Native American Consultation Database
www.cast.uark.edu/other/nps/nacd

National Center for Injury Prevention and Control
www.cdc.gov/ncipc

Northwest AIDS Education and Training Center Tribal BEAR Project
http://depts.washington.edu/nwaetc/

Indian Health Services
www.ihs.gov

Indigenous Peoples Task Force
www.indigenouspeoplestf.org

Mending the Sacred Hoop
www.msh-ta.org

Websites

Native American Children's Alliance
www.nativechildalliance.org

Hopi Cultural Preservation Office
www.nau.edu/~hcpo-p/

National Indian Child Welfare Association
www.nicwa.org

National Indian Health Board
www.nihb.org

National Native American AIDS Prevention Center
www.nnaapc.org/

Justice Department's Violence against Women Office
www.ojp.usdoj.gov/vawo

Tribal Law and Policy Institute
www.tribal-institute.org

Urban Indian Health Institute
www.uihi.org

Videos

It Can Happen to Anybody. Produced by the Native American Women's Health Education Resource Center, 1997, Video (15 min.)

Bitter Earth: Child Sexual Abuse in Indian Country. Office for Victims of Crime, 1993, Video.

B.J. Learns about Federal & Tribal Court. Office for Victims of Crime, 1992, Video.

In the Light of Reverence. Bullfrog Films, Video (73 min.).

White Shaman and Plastic Medicine Men. Native Voices, PBS Video (25 min.).

Hopi: Songs of the Fourth World. New Day Films, Video (60 min.).

Index

Index

Edelson, Jeffrey D., 55

Faller, Kathleen Colburn, 63
Ferguson, F.N., 19
Firethunder, Cecilia, 57
Frank, Michael D., 55
Frist, Bill, 6

Geronimo, 3
God is Red (Deloria), 82
Government-to-government relationships
and cultural places, 86, 88–92, 94
and health care, 11
and religion, 72–75
Gregory, Martha, 58

Halsey, Theresa, 49
Health issues, 2–3, 43, 50
access to care, 9–10, 33, 37, 60, 106
care, 6–11
causes of death, 4, 6, 8, 12–23
ceremonies, 7
funding, 8, 31
history, 7–11
HIV/AIDS, 24–42
and poverty, 23–24, 29
prevention resources, 10, 13
Heart to Heart Children's Advocacy
Center, 64–65
HIV/AIDS, 2–3, 25
prevention measures, 26, 29, 33–39
transmission factors, 27–35, 40–42
Hootch, Lynn, 57–58
Horn, JoAnn, 58

IHS. *See* Indian Health Service
Indian Health Care Improvement Act
(1976), 9
Indian Health Service (IHS), 28, 32
Indian Self-Determination and
Education Assistance Act (1975), 9
Indigenous peoples task force, 37
Influenza, 10

Jefferson, Thomas, 97
Johnson, Alan, 102

Kameroff, Priscilla, 58
King, Thomas, 101

Lyons, Oren, 5, 76

Mankiller, Wilma, 5
May, Philip, 16
Meriam Report, 8

NACA. *See* Native American Children's
Alliance
NAGPRA. *See* Native American Graves
Protection and Repatriation Act
National Congress of American
Indians, 96
National Environmental Policy Act
(NEPA), 93–94, 102
National Historic Preservation Act,
103–5
National Indian Child Welfare
Association (NICWA), 65–66
National Indian Health Board (NIHB),
13
National Native American AIDS
Prevention Center (NNAPC), 25
programs, 26, 35–36
publications, 36
Native American Children's Alliance
(NACA), 65–66
Native American Graves Protection
and Repatriation Act (NAGPRA)
purpose, 86–88, 96–98
Native Americans
diversity, 3, 53–54
modern social issues of, 1–5, 106
population, 11
worldview, 38, 49–50, 93, 99–100
NEPA. *See* National Environmental
Policy Act
NICWA. *See* National Indian Child
Welfare Association
NIHB. *See* National Indian Health
Board

Index

Picture Credits

page:

4: AP/Wide World Photos
20: © Reuters/CORBIS
27: AP/Wide World Photos
40: © Bob Rowan; Progressive
Images/CORBIS
46: © CORBIS
58: Courtesy of Sacred Circle,

National Resource Center to End
Violence Against Native Women
74: © Bettmann/CORBIS
78: © Getty Images
90: AP/Wide World Photos
100: © Bill Ross/CORBIS

Roe W. Bubar, J.D., is Associate Professor at the Center for Applied Studies in American Ethnicity (CASAE) and the School of Social Work at Colorado State University. Her expertise lies in the areas of American Indian law, violence against Native women, and child sexual abuse in Indian Country and Alaska Native communities. Bubar has written articles that have appeared in *Wicazo Sa Review* and *Social Justice*, and a chapter, along with coauthor Irene Vernon, titled: "Native Perspective on Teaching Law and U.S. Policy: The Inclusion of Federal Indian Law and Policy in College Curriculum," which appears in *Teaching Diversity: Challenges and Complexities, Identities and Integrity*.

Irene S. Vernon, Ph.D., is Associate Professor of English and is the Director of the Center for Applied Studies in American Ethnicity (CASAE) at Colorado State University. She has taught courses on various aspects of Native life and culture, including religion, law, history, literature, and economic development. Vernon has published a book, *Killing Us Quietly: Native Americans and HIV/AIDS* (2001), and has written articles that have appeared in the *American Indian Culture and Research Journal, American Indian Quarterly*, and *Wicazo Sa Review*.

Paul C. Rosier received his Ph.D. in American History from the University of Rochester, with a specialty in Native American History. His first book, *Rebirth of the Blackfeet Nation, 1912–1954*, was published by the University of Nebraska Press in 2001. In November 2003, Greenwood Press published *Native American Issues* as part of its Contemporary American Ethnic Issues series. Dr. Rosier has also published articles on Native American topics in the *American Indian Culture and Research Journal*, and the *Journal of American Ethnic History*. In addition, he was coeditor of *The American Years: A Chronology of United States History*. He is Assistant Professor of History at Villanova University, where he also serves as a faculty advisor to the Villanova Native American Student Association.

Walter Echo-Hawk is a member of the Pawnee tribe. He is a staff attorney of the Native American Rights Fund (*www.narf.org*) and a Justice on the Supreme Court of the Pawnee Nation (*www.pawneenation.org/court*). He has handled cases and legislation affecting Native American rights in areas such as religious freedom, education, water rights, fishing rights, grave protection, and tribal repatriation of Native dead.